I0128130

THE INDO-PACIFIC REGION: SECURITY DYNAMICS AND CHALLENGES

THE INDO-PACIFIC REGION: SECURITY DYNAMICS AND CHALLENGES

Editors

Group Captain Sharad Tewari, VM (Retd)

Dr Roshan Khanijo

(Established 1870)

United Service Institution of India
New Delhi

Vij Books India Pvt Ltd
New Delhi (India)

Published by

Vij Books India Pvt Ltd
(Publishers, Distributors & Importers)
2/19, Ansari Road
Delhi – 110 002
Phones: 91-11-43596460, 91-11-47340674
Fax: 91-11-47340674
e-mail: vijbooks@rediffmail.com

Copyright © 2016, United Service Institution of India, New Delhi

ISBN (Pb): 9789385563317 (2016)

All rights reserved.

No part of this book may be reproduced, stored in a retrieval system, transmitted or utilized in any form or by any means, electronic, mechanical, photocopying, recording or otherwise, without the prior permission of the copyright owner. Application for such permission should be addressed to the publisher.

The views expressed in the book are of authors/contributors and not necessarily those of the USI or publishers.

Contents

PART– II

Dynamics of Cooperation, Competition and Conflict in the Indian Ocean

PART – III

Dynamics of Cooperation, Competition and Conflict in the Western Pacific

PART - IV

Measures for Forging Indo-Pacific Security Cooperation

Participants

General VK Singh, PVSM, AVSM, YSM (Retd)

Hon'ble Minister of State (Independent Charge) for Statistics and Programme Implementation, Minister of State for External Affairs and Overseas Indian Affairs

General Vijay Kumar Singh, PVSM, AVSM, YSM (Retd) was born on 10 May 1951. An alumnus of Birla Public School, Pilani and National Defence Academy, he served as the 26th Chief of Army Staff of the Indian Army.

Military Career

General Singh was commissioned into the 2nd Battalion of The Rajput Regiment (Kali Chindi) on 14 June 1970. He is a graduate of the Defence Services Staff College, Wellington with a competitive vacancy. He is also a graduate of US Army Rangers Course at Fort Benning, USA and US Army War College, Carlisle, Pennsylvania.

General Singh was awarded Yudh Seva Medal (YSM) for operations as part of IPKF in Sri Lanka, the Ati Vishisht Seva Medal (AVSM) for distinguished service while commanding a counter-insurgency force in 2005 and Param Vishisht Seva Medal (PVSM) in recognition of his exceptional and distinguished services in the Eastern Theatre in 2009.

He became Chief of Army Staff on 31 March 2010 and retired from the position on 31 May 2012.

Honours and Awards

On 11 March 2011, General Singh was inducted into the United States Army War College (Class of 2001 graduate) International Fellows Hall of Fame. He is the 33rd International Fellow and the first Indian Armed Forces officer to be inducted. He is a recipient of Param Vishisht Seva Medal, Ati Vishisht Seva Medal, Yudh Seva Medal and Ranger Tab.

Political Career

General Singh joined the Bhartiya Janata Party on 1 March 2014 and successfully contested Lok Sabha election from Ghaziabad constituency (2.4 million plus electorate). Presently, he is Minister of State (Independent Charge) for Statistics and Programme Implementation, Minister of State for External Affairs and Minister of State for Overseas Indian Affairs. As Minister of State for External Affairs, General Singh has represented India at several bilateral and multilateral events as well as Special Assignments in Asia, Africa, Latin America & the Caribbean region and Europe. "Courage and Conviction", his highly acclaimed autobiography, has been widely read in India. General Singh is married to Mrs. Bharti Singh and they have two daughters.

Vice Admiral Satish Soni, PVSM, AVSM, NM, ADC

Vice Admiral Satish Soni, PVSM, AVSM, NM, ADC is the Flag Officer Commanding-in-Chief, Eastern Naval Command since 16 Jun 2014. Before this appointment, he served as the Flag Officer Commanding-in-Chief Southern Naval Command.

The Admiral is an alumnus of the National Defence Academy and was commissioned into the Indian Navy on 01 July 1976. A specialist in Navigation and Aircraft Direction, the Flag Officer is an alumnus of the Defence Services Staff College, Wellington and College of Naval Warfare, Mumbai.

He has held various important command and staff appointments in his career. Sea commands include the ocean going minesweeper Kakinada, the guided missile corvette Kirpan, the guided missile frigate Talwar and the guided missile destroyer Delhi. He has had the honour of having commissioned two warships, Kakinada and Talwar, in Russia, as the Commanding Officer. His staff appointments include Deputy Director of Personnel, Joint Director of Naval Plans and Naval Assistant to Chief of the Naval Staff at IHQ MoD (Navy).

On elevation to Flag rank, Vice Admiral Satish Soni assumed responsibilities as the Assistant Chief of Personnel (Human Resource Development) at IHQ, MOD (Navy). Subsequently, he commanded the Eastern Fleet of the Indian Navy, and thereafter took over as Chief of Staff, Eastern Naval Command. He then was Commandant, National Defence Academy at Khadakvasla, Pune, before moving to New Delhi as the Deputy Chief of the Naval Staff at Integrated Headquarters MoD (Navy). He is a keen sportsman and has represented the Indian Navy in Squash and Golf.

Lt Gen PK Singh, PVSM, AVSM (Retd)

Lt Gen P K Singh was commissioned as a 2/Lt in the Indian Army in 1967. He retired as an Army Commander (C-in-C) in 2008. He is a graduate of the Defence Services Staff College, Wellington, the Higher Command Course and the National Defence College. His academic qualifications include MSc, M.Phil and Post-graduate Diploma in Business Management.

He took over as Director of the United Service Institution of India in January 2009. He is a member of the Governing Council of the Indian Council of World Affairs, New Delhi, and also member of the International Advisory Board of the RUSI International, London.

Vice Admiral Arun Kumar Singh, PVSM, AVSM, NM (Retd)

Vice Admiral Arun Kumar Singh retired from the Indian Navy in 2007, after over 40 years in naval uniform, as the Flag Officer Commanding in Chief of the Eastern Naval Command. He is an alumnus of the National Defence Academy Kharakvasla, the Defence Services Staff College (Wellington), College of Naval Warfare (Karanja), National Defence College (New Delhi), Admiral Frunze Academy (St Petersburg) and Admiral Makarov Academy (Vladivostok). He specialized in conventional & nuclear submarines, navigation and underwater launched missiles.

In addition to command of submarines and warships, he has held the appointments of ACNS (Submarines), Flag Officer Submarines and Flag Officer Commanding Eastern Fleet after promotion to flag rank. He has also been Controller of Personnel Services at IHQ MoD (Navy), Director General of the Indian Coast Guard, C-in-C Andaman & Nicobar Command and finally FOC-in-C, Eastern Naval Command. He has exercised with almost all Navies and Coast Guards of the Indian Ocean and Asia Pacific regions.

He participated in the 1971 Indo-Pak war and also served on active duty in Sri Lanka twice, the first time during the JVP insurgency in 1971 and later with the Indian Peace Keeping Force in 1989. He has been awarded the Param Vishisht Seva Medal, Ati Vishsht Seva Medal and Nao Sena Medal. Post retirement, the Admiral is a life member of the USI and National Maritime Foundation. He is a prolific writer and speaker on maritime and nuclear issues as well as on international affairs and has addressed various institutions in India and abroad.

Maj Gen Liu Chao (Retd)

Born in Liaoning, China, on 6 March 1959, Maj Gen Chao Liu (Retd) has nearly 40 years of military experience. He was the Force Commander of the United Nations Peacekeeping Force in Cyprus (UNFICYP) since 2011. Before that, he was the Military, Air and Naval Attaché at the Embassy of China in India from 2009 to 2011. His military experience includes command of a mechanized infantry division, command of a regiment, Section Chief in charge of Planning and Coordination, and Staff Officer in the PLA HQ in Beijing. In 1993-1994, he served in the United Nations Mission for the Referendum in Western Sahara as a military observer.

Maj Gen Liu Chao (Retd) has studied in Military Academy, Staff College and National Defence University. He holds a Master of Science degree from the London School of Economics and Political Science. He is currently the Senior Advisor, China Institute for International Strategic Studies (CIISS).

Vice Admiral Anurag Gopalam Thapliyal, AVSM &Bar (Retd)

Vice Admiral Anurag Gopalam Thapliyal, AVSM & Bar (Retd) is an alumnus of the Naval Academy (Silver medalist) and was commissioned into the Indian Navy on 01 Jul 1977. He is a Post Graduate in Physics from the University of Lucknow. He is an alumnus of the American Naval War College at Newport and the Defence Services Staff College at Wellington. He possesses two Masters Degrees, in Physics and Defence Studies, and has been awarded the Ati Vishist Seva Medal for distinguished service twice, in 2010 and 2014.

The Admiral has commanded four Surface combatants including the ASW corvette INS Ajay, the indigenous missile corvette INS Khukri, the stealth frigate INS Tabar (for which he was the commissioning Commanding Officer) and the indigenous destroyer INS Mysore. His last afloat appointment was command of the Indian Navy's Eastern Fleet.

He has also held various key staff appointments, including the Assistant Chief of Naval Staff (Operations and Information Warfare), Chief of Staff of the Eastern Naval Command, Commandant of the newly created Indian Naval Academy at Ezhimala and Chief of Personnel at IHQ MoD (Navy). He was appointed Director General of Indian Coast Guard in Feb 2013 and retired from the Naval Service on 31 Jan 2015.

Rear Admiral K Raja Menon (Retd)

Rear Admiral Menon was a career officer and a submarine specialist in the Navy and retired in 1994 as the Assistant Chief of Naval Staff (Operations). A prolific writer, his published work includes *Maritime Strategy and Continental Wars'*, a standard text for the Staff College. His second book *'A Nuclear Strategy for India'* is recommended reading for the Indian Strategic Forces. His third book *'The Indian Navy: A Photo Essay'* is the official gift of the navy. Other works include the edited book *'Weapons of Mass Destruction: Options for India;* an Occasional Paper, *The US-India Non-proliferation Divide: the Way Ahead* by Cooperative Monitoring Center, Sandia in 2005; *The Long View from Delhi: The Grand Strategy of Indian Foreign Policy* published in India and in USA in 2010.

Admiral Menon was a member of the Arun Singh Committee and of the National Defence University Committee. He is a visiting lecturer at all institutes of higher study of the Indian Armed Forces and the Foreign Office. He headed the group that recently wrote the Indian Navy's New Maritime Strategy, and recently retired as the Chairman of the Task Force on Net Assessment and Simulation in the National Security Council. He is a distinguished fellow in the Institute of Peace and Conflict Studies and the National Maritime Foundation.

His current areas of specialization are Nuclear Strategy; Maritime Strategy; Net Assessment and Strategic Scenarios, both Politico-Military and Technological; and Politico-Military Simulation and Gaming.

Ambassador Gleb Aleksandrovitch Ivashentsov

Ambassador Gleb Aleksandrovitch Ivashentsov is the Deputy Head of the Russian Center for APEC Studies with the diplomatic rank of Ambassador Extraordinary and Plenipotentiary. He graduated in 1967 from the International Economic Relations Faculty, Moscow State Institute of International Relations, and in 1991 from the Russian Diplomatic Academy. A polyglot, he can read Russian, English and Hindi and fluently speaks German and French.

During his long and illustrious career, he has been Consul General of USSR/ Russia in Bombay from 1991-1995, Ambassador of Russia to Myanmar from 1997-2001 and Ambassador of Russia to the Republic of Korea from 2005-2009.

Ambassador Ivashentsov has been conferred state awards, namely 'The Order of Friendship' (Russia) in 2003 and 'Khanhwa Medal for Diplomatic Merits' (Republic of Korea) in 2009.

Among his acclaimed publications include "India". His most recent publications in Russian are *India – Basics in Brief* (2009) and *Behind the Fortifications of 38th Parallel* (2012). In the Korean language, he has authored *The Other Korea* (Seoul, 2012) and in English The *Tiger of the Land of Morning Calm* (New Delhi, 2014). He has also been Special Research Fellow at the China Center for Contemporary World Studies.

Dr Mumin Chen

Mumin Chen, PhD is an Associate Professor and Chair of the Graduate Institute of International Politics as well as Director of the Centre for Strategic Studies on South Asia and the Middle East at the National Chung Hsing University, Taichung, Taiwan. His research focuses on international security theory, Chinese foreign policy, Taiwan-China relations and regional politics and security in South Asia. Chen has published six books: *International Security Theory: Power, State and Threat* (in Chinese, 2009), *Prosperity but Insecurity: Globalization and China's National Security 1979-2000*(2010), *International Relations Illustrated* (in Chinese, co-author with Chen Wan-yu, 2012), *Movies and International Relations* (in Chinese, co-author with Chen Fong-yu,2014), *India and China in the Emerging Dynamics of East Asia* (co-edited with GVC Naidu and Raviprasad Narayanan, 2015), and *New Perspectives on South Asia* (in Chinese, co-edited with William A. Stanton, 2015).

Professor Yang Minghong

Professor Yang Minghong is currently the Executive Director of the Faculty of Social Development and Western China Studies at Sichuan University. His educational background includes Bachelor's and Master's degrees in History from Sichuan University, a doctorate from Sichuan University and post-doctoral work at the South-western University of Finance and Economics. His research areas include Tibetan Studies, Macroeconomics, Regional Studies, Agricultural economics and management, and Tibetan economic and social development. He has a number of published articles to his credit.

Vice Admiral Anil Kumar Chopra, PVSM, AVSM (Retd)

Vice Admiral Anil Chopra was commissioned into the Indian Navy on 01 July 1975 and retired on 31 March 2015 as the Flag Officer Commanding-in-Chief, Western Naval Command. He is one of only two Admirals in the Indian Navy who have headed both operational commands, having commanded the Eastern Naval Command from October 2011 till June 2014. He was appointed Director General of the Indian Coast Guard just a few days after the 26/11 terror attack on Mumbai in November 2008.

He has a brilliant academic record, having topped every course he underwent throughout his career. He is a graduate of the National Defence Academy, Kharakvasla; the Defence Services Staff College, Wellington; the Naval War College, Rhode Island and the National Defence College, New Delhi. He is the recipient of the 'Binoculars' for being the best Naval Cadet, the Sword of Honour as the best all-round Midshipman, the Admiral RD Katari Trophy for heading the Long Gunnery Course, the Scudder Medal at DSSC and the Colonel Pyarelal Medal at the NDC.

His seagoing commands include the missile corvette INS Kuthar, the missile destroyer INS Rajput and the Aircraft Carrier, INS Viraat and command of the prestigious Western Fleet. Important shore assignments include being the Director of Naval Plans and later the Assistant Chief of Naval Staff (Policy and Plans) at IHQ MoD (Navy) and the Chief of Staff, Eastern Naval Command. His experience abroad includes being stationed at Rome, Italy for nearly three years in the 1980s in connection with the induction of combat systems for frontline units, and being a Senior Fellow at the United States Atlantic Council. For his distinguished service to the nation, he was awarded the Ati Vishisht Seva Medal in 2007 and the Param Vishisht Seva Medal in 2013.

Lt Gen Datuk Azizan Bin Md Delin

Lieutenant General Datuk Azizan Bin Md Delin was born on 23th February 1960 and joined the Malaysian Armed Forces in 1979, being awarded the sword of honour on commissioning. He holds a Degree in Law (Honours) from MARA University of Technology and Master's Degree in International Security and Civil Military Relations from the Naval Post Graduate School, Monterey, California, USA. In 2015, he has attended the Senior Program of Harvard Kennedy School at the Harvard University. He has also attended various military courses locally and abroad.

His military experience includes appointments such as the Commanding Officer of a military unit, Commandant at Malaysian Royal Military College, Commander of The Eighth Infantry Brigade Malaysia, Human Resources Director, Commander of the Second Infantry Division, and Chief of Personnel Staff of the Malaysian

Armed Forces. Prior to his current appointment, he was the Assistant Chief of Staff of the Personnel Services Division, Malaysian Armed Forces Headquarters. He was appointed as the Chief Executive of the Malaysian Institute of Defence and Security in August 2015.

Commodore Lalit Kapur (Retd)

Commodore Lalit Kapur was commissioned into the Indian Navy in 1975. He is a specialist in Navigation and Aircraft Direction. The Commodore was a member of the Fifth Indian Scientific Expedition to Antarctica where he pioneered a technique for survey of the Ice Shelf in the vicinity of Dakshin Gangotri.

An alumnus of the Defence Services Staff College, Wellington, he also served as the Directing Staff there. He underwent Long Defence Management Course (LDMC) at College of Defence Management Secunderabad and then served as Directing Staff at the College of Naval Warfare, Mumbai. He was Defence Adviser, Embassy of India, Muscat, with concurrent accreditation to the UAE, Qatar and Bahrain. Other important assignments include being the first Deputy Assistant Chief of Integrated Defence Staff (Defence Protocol and Foreign Liaison) in the Defence Intelligence Agency at HQ IDS, Principal Direct (Systems) in the Strategic Forces Command and Chief Staff Officer (Operations) at Headquarters Offshore Defence Advisory Group, Mumbai. His sea experience includes a range of both Western and Eastern origin warships, command of an Oceangoing Minesweeper and the 19th Mine Counter Measures Squadron. He was also the second-in-command of INS Vikrant and officiated in command for over 10 months. A prolific reader of international relations and military history, Commodore Lalit Kapur has a number of published articles to his credit.

Shri Ranjit Singh Kalha, IFS (Retd)

Ambassador Ranjit Singh Kalha joined the Indian Foreign Service in 1965. After holding the key posts of Joint Secretary (Americas) and Joint Secretary (East Asia), he became Additional Secretary (Administration) and Secretary (West) in the Ministry of External Affairs. He served as India's Ambassador to Indonesia and Iraq. On superannuation,

Ambassador Kalha was appointed by the President of India as Member, National Human Rights Commission with rank equivalent to Judge, Supreme Court of India.

The Canadian House of Commons honoured Ambassador Kalha on 14 June 2001 with a citation for his services in the promotion of Indo-Canadian relations.

An alumnus of Punjab University and University of Hong Kong, Ambassador Kalha is fluent in Chinese and led the Indian side for the India-China Boundary Sub-Group negotiations from 1985 to 1988. Having lived and worked in China, a greater part of Ambassador Kalha's career was spent in handling Chinese affairs.

Ambassador Kalha has authored three books; *The Ultimate Prize- -Saddam and Oil, The Dynamics of Preventive Diplomacy and India-China Boundary Issues–Quest for Settlement.* He is a well- known commentator on Chinese affairs and on the politics of oil. He appears regularly on national TV and has contributed several articles to both the international and national media.

Col Nguyen The Hong

Born in 1972, Colonel Nguyen The Hong joined the Vietnam People's Army in 1990 after graduating from high school. On completion of his initial training in 1995, he was appointed as Research Assistant in Vietnam's Institute for Defense Strategic Studies (IDSS) from 1995 to 2000 and thereafter as Research Assistant in Institute for Defence International Relations (IDIR) from 2001 to 2005. He was the Deputy Defence Attaché of Vietnam to China from 2009 to 2012. In February, 2013, he was appointed as Head of Asia-African Division of IDIR and holds this position till date.

Col Nguyen The Hong has successfully qualified training courses in colleges in the Army and abroad including at the Military College of Foreign Languages in 1991-1995; at the Academy of Military Science 2001-2003; China's Peking University in 2006-2007. He was awarded a Master's Degree at China's University for Political Science and Law (Zhong Guo Zheng fa Da Xue) in 2012. He speaks both English and Chinese fluently.

Captain (Navy) Sukjoon Yoon (Retd)

Captain Sukjoon Yoon (Retd) is currently a senior research fellow of the Korea Institute for Maritime Strategy (KIMS). Before joining KIMS, Captain Yoon's more than thirty years of commissioned service included thirteen years at sea as surface warfare officer and several command and staff appointments. He has been Director of Maritime Strategy Studies at the Naval War College, senior lecturer, Naval Academy, Commanding Officer of ROKS WONSAN, Director of Policy Division, ROKN Headquarters and adjunct professor of the Centre for Chinese Studies, IFANS, MOFAT, Seoul, Korea. He is a graduate of the Naval Academy class of 1976 and of the Commander's Course of the Naval War College in Korea. He holds a MA in Chinese politics from *Fu Hsing Kang* Institute of the National Defense University, Taiwan and a Ph. D in international politics from Bristol University United Kingdom. He is an executive member of the SLOC-Study Group-Korea and advisory member of the National Diplomatic Academy of Korea. He has written on a broad range of Asian Maritime Security issues. His recent works include Sukjoon Yoon, 'The Abe's Apology: A South Korean Perspective,' *The Diplomat*, 23 August 2015; Sukjoon Yoon, 'China's WW2 Ceremony: Why President Park is Attending,' *RSIS Commentary*, No 136, 28 August, 2015; Sukjoon Yoon, "Implications of Xi Jinping's True Maritime Power: Its Context, Significance, and Impact on the Region," U.S. *Naval War College Review*, Vol. 68, No. 3, Summer 2015.

Dr Huang Yunsong

Professor Huang Yunsong is currently an Assistant Professor in the Faculty of Social Development and Western China Development Studies at Sichuan University. His educational background includes Bachelor's and Master's degrees in Law from Sichuan University, a doctorate from Sichuan University and post-doctoral work at the University of Michigan. His research areas include Public International Law, International Studies, South Asian Studies and Refugee and Asylum Law. He has a number of published articles to his credit.

Dr Chi-shin Chang

Dr Chi-shin Chang earned his Bachelor's Degree in International Relations; his Master's Degree in Chinese Diplomatic History, National Security Studies and Theories of International Politics; and his Doctorate in International Relations, specialising in International Security, Ethnic Conflict, Conflict Resolution and East Asia Security Studies from the National Cheng-chi University, Taipei, Taiwan. His work experience includes being an Assistant Research Fellow at Taiwan Research Institute, a Research Fellow at Taiwan Foundation for Democracy, a lecturer for diplomatic personnel at Taiwan Knowledge Base Corporation, a Post-doctoral Research Fellow, and Adjunct Assistant Professor in the Centre for General Education and an Assistant Research Fellow in the Centre for Asia Policy, the last three at the National Tsing-Hua University, Hsin-chu, Taiwan.

Dr Chang has over 30 published papers/articles/symposium papers/book chapters and technical reports to his credit.

Shri Sanjay Singh, IFS (Retd)

Ambassador Sanjay Singh is an alumnus of Delhi University, from where obtained a Master's degree in Physics. He joined the Indian Foreign Service in 1976 and served in Indian Missions in Mexico, Germany, Ghana and France and in the Ministry of External Affairs, New Delhi. He was Director in the Office of the External Affairs Minister and Joint Secretary and Head of Division dealing with Latin American Countries. From October 1997 to June 2001, he was India's Consul General in Ho Chi Minh City and from July 2001 to August 2004, Deputy Chief of Mission in Paris. He held charge in the Ministry as Joint Secretary and Additional Secretary (Gulf) from March 2005 to March 2009. He was India's Ambassador to Iran from March 2009 to March 2011. He took over as Secretary (East) in the Ministry of External Affairs in March 2011 and retired in end April 2013.

Lt Gen Mollah Fazle Akbar (Retd)

Lieutenant General Mollah Fazle Akbar was commissioned in the Corps of Artillery on 30 November 1976. He took over as the Commandant,

National Defence College (NDC), Bangladesh, on 24 June 2011. Lieutenant General Akbar is a Freedom Fighter and participated in the War of Independence of Bangladesh in 1971. He is also the Colonel Commandant of the Regiment of Artillery of Bangladesh Army since 2010.

As staff, he worked as the Brigade Major of two Infantry Brigades, Staff Officer in Directorate General of Forces Intelligence (DGFI), Grade One Staff Officer (Training & Operations) in an Infantry Division, Assistant Defence Adviser at Bangladesh High Commission in India and Colonel Staff in an Infantry Division. He also performed as Director of Military Operations and Director of Artillery in General Staff Branch, Army Headquarters.

Lieutenant General Akbar commanded an Air Defence Artillery Unit. He also commanded the only Air Defence Artillery Brigade (ADA) of Bangladesh Army and a Field Artillery Brigade. He also commanded a Sector of the then Bangladesh Rifles, present Border Guard Bangladesh (BGB). He was also a Sector Commander of UN Peace Keeping Force in UNMIL (United Nations Mission in Liberia). Before his current assignment at NDC, he was the Chief of Defence Intelligence of Bangladesh as the Director General of Directorate General of Forces Intelligence (DGFI).

He attended a number of courses both at home and abroad. He attended Anti-Aircraft Firing Drone Course from China and Security Intelligence Administration Course from United Kingdom. He earned his Masters of Philosophy (M.Phil.) from National University of Bangladesh.

Dr Victor Sumsky

Dr Victor Sumsky is Director of the ASEAN Centre in MGIMO University of Moscow, an author of three monographs and numerous articles published in Russia as well as in the US, China, India, Indonesia, South Korea, Malaysia, Singapore and the Philippines. In the past he worked for the Soviet Foreign Ministry, Institute of Oriental Studies and Institute of World Economy and International Relations (IMEMO) in Moscow. His overseas work experience includes the University of the Philippines, London School of Economics, and the University of Washington. From 2004 to 2010 Dr Sumsky represented Russia on the Board of the European Association of Southeast Asian Studies (Euro-SEAS). He is a member of CSCAP, Russia. The primary areas of his professional interests are political development of Southeast Asian nations, ASEAN's history and present-day problems, international relations and regional security in East Asia.

Along with Mark Hong and Amy Lugg, Victor Sumsky is a co-editor of "ASEAN-Russia: Foundations and Future Prospects" (Singapore, 2012, 376 p.) jointly published by MGIMO University and the Institute of Southeast Asian Studies (ISEAS) to commemorate the 15th Anniversary of ASEAN-Russia Dialogue Partnership. In 2015, Dr. Sumsky contributed to a forecast entitled "Russia and the World in 2020: An Outline of a Troubled Future" (Moscow, 384 p., in Russian).

Dr Michael Pillsbury

Michael Pillsbury (Chinese: 白邦瑞) is a Pentagon adviser, former government official and author of three books on China: *Chinese Views of Future Warfare, China Debates the Future Security Environment and The One Hundred Year Marathon: China's Secret Strategy.*

During the Reagan administration, Pillsbury was the head of Pentagon Policy Planning. He was responsible for implementation of the program of covert aid to Afghanistan and elsewhere known as the Reagan Doctrine. In 1975-76, while an analyst at the RAND Corporation, Pillsbury published articles in *Foreign Policy* and *International Security* recommending that the United States establish intelligence and military ties with China. The proposal, publicly commended by Ronald Reagan, Henry Kissinger and James Schlesinger, later became US policy during the Carter and Reagan administrations. In 1992, under President George H. W. Bush, Pillsbury was Special Assistant for Asian Affairs in the Office of the Secretary of Defense, reporting to Andrew W. Marshall, Director of Net Assessment. Pillsbury is a member of the Council on Foreign Relations and the International Institute for Strategic Studies.

Commander MH Rajesh

Cdr MH Rajesh is an alumnus of Naval Academy and Defence Services Staff College. He has over two decades of experience in the Indian Navy. He has tenured various operational and staff assignments including command of a Submarine. He has post graduate degrees in History from Mumbai University and Strategic Studies from Madras University. He is presently a Research Fellow at United Service Institution of India, focusing on China and Indian Ocean.

Introduction

Lieutenant General PK Singh, PVSM, AVSM (Retd)

The Indo-Pacific Region: Security Dynamics and Challenges

Asia – the birthplace of numerous civilisations, the centre of world political and economic affairs till colonised in the 17th and 18th centuries and the neglected 'other side of the world' during the Cold War period has increasingly assumed centre stage in global political discourse. By far the world's largest continent, Asia comprises 49 different states spread over nearly 44.6 million Km^2, around 30 per cent of earth's total land area. Its population has already crossed the 4.4 billion mark, constitutes about 60 per cent of the world population and is projected to cross 5 billion by 2050. Gone are the days when Asia depended on the West even for food; today it is an agricultural and industrial powerhouse. In PPP terms, Asia's GDP is already more than 30 percent of world GDP; is projected to cross 40 percent by 2023 and comprise over half the world GDP by 2050. Japan, South Korea and China are already technology centers and India has made its presence felt in the software domain. No wonder that the world talks of the 21st Century as Asia's Century and Australia sees its future as inextricably linked to Asia.

Territorial expanse, manpower, technology and economic heft all put Australasia in the front ranks of the globe. But the region's diversity in culture, ethnicity, religions, ideology, environment, history, economy and systems of governance is without parallel. Consequently, conflict is endemic. As of today, Asia is 'ground zero' for several ongoing or potential conflicts including, inter alia, the war on terror in the Af-Pak region, state sponsored export of Jihadi terror from Pakistan, the Shia-Sunni Conflict in Yemen and the Levant, the Arab-Israeli Conflict, territorial disputes in the South and East China Seas, the Taiwan issue and the North Korean imbroglio. These 'hot spots' generate instability that inevitably impacts geopolitically and economically on the entire continent, indeed, the entire world, affecting energy and trade flows, creating religious divides, causing acute humanitarian distress, displacing entire populations. Add to this worry about nuclear weapons falling into terrorist hands, particularly given Pakistan's opaque nuclear doctrine, refusal to consider NFU and thrust towards tactical nuclear weapons. Managing this cocktail of conflict and instability is, therefore, an overriding global priority.

Going hand in hand with conflict is multi-faceted competition. At one level, it is for resources: the emerging economies of the Asia Pacific, South and South East Asia compete for energy and mineral resources with developed countries, including USA, Europe, Japan and South Korea. The Middle East has nearly 50% of the world's proven reserves of petroleum and 40 percent of the reserves of natural gas. More important, it has the biggest exportable surplus of both. Asia and Africa have enormous resources of the other vital and much sought minerals and ores. At another level, the competition is for markets, with growing economies competing amongst each other as well as with developed nations for market access and share. Of greater concern is geopolitical competition. The effective regional hegemon is USA, which would naturally like to preserve its primacy and has built up a network of alliances towards this end. The American maritime strategy of "Forward, engaged, ready" is intended to ensure that USA has the ability to quickly use military force in the Indo-Asia-Pacific region in conjunction with allies to pursue American objectives. China, however, perceives this alliance network as directed against it, intended to prevent its rise and hem it in; and has developed counter strategies like the Maritime Silk Route which creates infrastructure in Myanmar, Bangladesh, Sri Lanka, Pakistan and Africa that can be used militarily; as well as strengthening the PLAN and deploying it in the Indian Ocean. China has also developed common ground with Russia as well as Iran to counter perceived American dominance and alliances with Arab nations. At the same time, India perceives that China has hemmed it in with a 'string of pearls' and supports Pakistan as a rival to India, preventing natural growth into a possible regional rival. To India, Chinese forays into the Indian Ocean generate considerable concern. Pakistan, in turn, is concerned by India's rise and competes at many levels. Religious and ideological competitions add to complications.

Along with conflict and competition, cooperation has made its appearance, necessitated by both economic considerations as well as the numerous non-traditional challenges faced by the region, including natural disasters such as cyclones and droughts, earthquakes and tsunamis, floods and tidal surges; piracy in the vicinity of the Horn of Africa and the Malacca Straits; maritime terrorism such as the attacks on Mumbai in 2008; gun-running, smuggling, traffic in people, illicit migration and illegal fishing, as well as environmental pollution and the effects of global warming. These challenges have trans-national dimensions and are far beyond the ability of any one nation to deal with; cooperation is an essential pre-requisite to address them. This cooperation is presently sub-regional and issue based, with no overarching mechanism that gives Asia's inhabitants the prime voice in managing their affairs. Existing cooperative mechanisms are of varying effectiveness and appear divided both by the oceans as well as by who sponsors them. At the global level, the Asian Infrastructure Investment Bank (AIIB) has been launched by China with the stated objective of providing finance to infrastructure projects in Asia and has already attracted 57 prospective founding members. Some perceive it as a counter to the IMF, World Bank and Asian Development Bank, which are dominated by developed countries, as well as the opening move of a strategy designed to make the Yuan the world's reserve currency. The New Development Bank (NDB), formed in 2014, headquartered in Shanghai and operated by the BRICS is also perceived as a counter to the IMF and the World Bank. At the continental level, Western Pacific has APEC, the TPP, RCEP and many others; South East Asia has ASEAN, South Asia has SAARC, Central Asia has the SCO, the Arabian Peninsula has the GCC and the Indian

Ocean has IORA and the IONS. These mechanisms disaggregate Asia into West, South, South East, Central and East Asia from both economic and security perspectives, with little meeting ground between them.

Economic growth and continued development of Asia as a whole are contingent upon security and stability, without which precious resources will inevitably be expended in conflict. Security, however, is a grey area. The existing security system is a relic of the Cold War and dominated by USA, which has assumed responsibility of ensuring not only secure trade corridors, so vital for Asia's economic growth, but also regional security. Consequently, Asia's security is shaped primarily by American perceptions of what is required to protect their interests. The events of the last three decades have necessitated interventions in Afghanistan and Iraq, stretching even American capability. Although USA still remains by far the world's most powerful nation, there is an increasing appearance of fatigue, leading to doubt about America's ability and willingness to intervene in disputes that don't impinge directly on its own interests.

The willingness of Asian nations to continue letting America handle security concerns has many causes. First, the vision of most political leaders extends to the region of immediate concern to them, including nations with common land borders and in the extended neighbourhood. Second, security entails considerable cost. Resources, capability and capacity are limited, with other areas competing for priority. Third is a level of comfort with history and the colonial heritage, which divided Asia into different spheres of influence and left Asian nations dependent on external powers to manage their own security. Change is never easy, especially when it involves assuming the responsibility for your own security. Finally, it is due to the fact that the interests of Asian nations are incredibly diverse and meeting ground is difficult to find.

Over the last decade or so, however, the realisation has emerged that interests of Asia's rapidly developing economies intersect in the maritime domain. From a maritime perspective, Asia's Pacific Rim is inseparable from its Indian Ocean Rim. The maritime domain that connects sources of energy in West Asia and well as Asian Russia (or potential sources in the Arctic) with their primary markets in India, China, Japan and South Korea. It connects Asia's and Africa's primary resource providers with the consuming countries. It connects Asia's industrial producers including China, Australia, Japan, South Korea and India with their markets, in Asia, Africa, Europe and the Americas. The flow of global trade is predominantly over the seas; trade over land entails higher costs and is subject to greater uncertainties. The Indo-Pacific region is the world's busiest trade corridor, taking up more than 60% of global oil flows, over a third of all bulk traffic and over half of all container traffic. Finally, it permits easy access to hot spots as well as movement of military resources to deal with existing threats.

The continent's lynchpin is South-East Asia, connecting the Indian and the Pacific Oceans and linking the Middle-East and South Asia with the Asia Pacific and Australia. Talk of the maritime connect has been in the air for a few years now. Australia incorporated the term 'Indo-Pacific' into its 2013 white paper on defence and Australian leaders make no bones about their desire to see the emergence of an Indo-Pacific security mechanism. The American Maritime Strategy released in March 2015 talks of the Indo-Asia-Pacific region. Prime Minister Modi's engagement with Japan, China, Vietnam, Australia, and South Korea, coupled with his 'Act East' Policy are a pointer in the same direction.

Given the proven limitations of the UNSC in handling various situations, there is pressing need for a regional infrastructure to deal with security matters, including both traditional and non-traditional threats. It is for the nations whose interests are most affected to work together to build a comprehensive Pan Asian security mechanism, dispelling the apprehensions of the continent's inhabitants and creating the capability to handle their own affairs. Ideally, the mechanism must give primacy to regional views, taking into account the views of interested extra-regional powers, but without giving them primacy or overarching veto powers.

This book is based on the papers presented by various speakers at the 36th USI National Security Seminar on 19 and 20 November 2015. The USI took a conscious decision in the year 2009 to host an international seminar every November to look at the Indo-Pacific region. This was done because the world talked of 21st century being the century of Asia. So if there is going to be a century and we are going to look at the rise of Asia for next 100 years, then we need to study this phenomena. From a maritime perspective, the Asia's Pacific Rim is inseparable from the Indian Ocean Rim. So the Indo-Pacific region is therefore of great interest globally. That's the area where lot of things are happening and will continue to happen. This is the region in which we see cooperation, we see competition and we see conflict of interest. Economic growth is dependent on security and stability without which precious resources will inevitably be expended in conflict. Given the proven limitation of the UN Security Council, there is a need for a regional infrastructure to deal with traditional and non-traditional security threats.

The Keynote address to the seminar was delivered by General VK Singh, the Hon'ble Minister of State. Thereafter the seminar was conducted in four sessions. Each of the sessions was chaired by eminent personalities in this field. The speakers being from various countries, gave a true picture of the concerns of the affected nations. The Valedictory address was delivered by Vice Admiral Satish Soni.

The first session was chaired by Vice Admiral AK Singh and focused on 'The Indo-Pacific as a Geo-strategic Concept and Construct'. During this session five speakers presented their papers with the focus on Strategic and Geostrategic issues; Indo-Pacific Region as a Security Construct; Implications of the Maritime Silk Road (MSR): A Russian Perspective; China's Role as a Maritime Power and its Impact on Security Environment in East Asia and Indo-Pacific; and finally on China's MSR initiative in the context of IOR-Pacific Security and Economic Cooperation.

The second session was chaired by Vice Admiral AK Chopra and discussed issues on 'Dynamics of Cooperation, Competition and Conflict in the Indian Ocean'. Two speakers presented their papers on the Dynamics of Competition, Cooperation and Conflict in South East Asia and in the Middle East.

The third session was chaired by Ambassador RS Kalha and focused on Dynamics of Cooperation, Competition and Conflict in the Western Pacific. A total of four speakers presented their papers on Competition, Conflict and Cooperation and Challenges to the management of South China Sea situation; South Korean Perspective of the Conflict in East China Sea; Interplay between Security of the IOR and Dynamics in South China Sea; and Taiwan-China Relations: Risk or Opportunity for Peace in East Asia.

The fourth session was chaired by Ambassador Sanjay Singh and co-chaired by Lt Gen MF Akbar. This session discussed issues related to 'Measures for Forging Indo-Pacific Security Cooperation'. Three speakers presented their papers in the seminar on the subject issues. Some of the issues brought out by one of the speakers were not relevant for the seminar, these have been included in the book being his personal views and for the readers to judge its veracity.

During the course of the seminar quite a number of issues came about for discussion from the participants and the audience. Some of the important ones have been summarised in the conclusion. Overall, this book provides a comprehensive view of the perspectives of Security Dynamics and Challenges in the Indo-Pacific Region.

Keynote Address

General VK Singh, PVSM, AVSM,YSM (Retd)

Hon'ble Minister of State (Independent Charge) for Statistics and Programme Implementation, Minister of State for External Affairs and Overseas Indian Affairs

Introduction

The Director USI, Lt Gen PK Singh, General VN Sharma, our previous Army Chief, delegates from friendly foreign countries, senior serving officers and the retired senior fraternity which is present here, members of the USI Council, ladies and gentlemen.

It is a pleasure to be amongst you, especially to see so many people who have come for this very interesting seminar on Indo-Pacific Region: Security Dynamics and Challenges. Needless to say, that this is an important arena of foreign policy of India. It's an important arena for the think tanks to look at; it's an important arena for security specialists to look at and why I say it is an important arena for the foreign policy challenges that we face because, this is one area which is commercially and from security point of view important to us. I am sure you all are aware that in the 90s India embarked on what was termed at that time as the 'Look East' policy. Our whole aim was that we should look at what is to our East and how beneficial it is to us and how to integrate this area of importance to us. Today that 'Look East', with the new government which came in last year and our Prime Minister advocated that 'Look East' into an 'Act East', because we found that I think we were looking more and not acting more. So today it is 'Act East' in which we not only look at our neighbourhood, we not only look at our own country's east and northeast, we also look at further into the Pacific. We are also, as you are aware, members of the IORA, the Indian Ocean Rim Association of countries, in which we look at how this impacts various things and how we can cooperate for betterment of various interests in this region. Primarily, India Ocean Rim countries look at how to exploit the riches which are available in this for the benefit of all the member countries and what should be done to ensure that our security concerns remains addressed.

The Pacific Region

At the same time, we are also looking at the Pacific region. You are aware of the type of agreements and type of engagements that we have had with Australia, Japan and New Zealand and our aim has been that we need to look at the Pacific because both the Indian Ocean and the Pacific have serious concerns for us. When we look at the Pacific, recently we did have a seminar which was with the Pacific island countries, small island but important from strategic point of view. We had 14 nations which came in and there was a serious engagement with them in terms of how we can prove our usefulness and friendliness to these countries and therefore, India went on to extend not only the hands of friendship, we extended lines of credit, we ensured that there is a better understanding of each other's concerns in this area. There were some who were not so well versed in matters security like you all who questioned us as to what India was doing with the Pacific island countries. But you would understand why it is important to have island countries in the Pacific, along with important land mass that is occupied by ASEAN countries, to be with us. To be looking at the way we see things and we understand what their concerns are.

ASEAN Connectivity

You are aware of the ASEAN summit that took place in Nay Pyi Taw which our Prime Minister (PM) attended and PM's concern was in terms of how to better our relations with ASEAN in all spheres. We talk of trade, we talk of connectivity and when I say connectivity, ladies and gentlemen, it's not just connectivity which is geographic; we are looking at connectivity which is geographic; we look at connectivity which is in terms of trade and commerce; we are looking at connectivity which brings academic institutions and think tanks together; and we are looking at connectivity which looks at cultural and religious aspects between ASEAN and India. And therefore, aim is to strengthen this bonding with ASEAN, not only in these issues but also security matters where we understand what their concerns are. And, I am quite sure that ASEAN would welcome India as a balancer in terms of various concerns that it has; various security challenges that they look at and looking at somebody who is benign and who is willing to help them in realizing their own potential in a more secured environment. So that has been our connectivity; our concern; our engagement with ASEAN countries and when you look from ASEAN downwards in to the Pacific you would realise why we engage so effectively with the Pacific island countries whom we had invited for a summit here in India.

India's Importance in the Region

What does all lead to? What it leads to is that, India as an important player because of its geographic location; India as an important player in terms of peace and harmony that it looks at; India as an important player which is looking at its own advancement by cooperating with various nations and that is why you have all those programmes which have been brought out 'Make in India'; 'Skilled India'; 'Digital India' where we are asking people to cooperate with us and which brings us to an important slot where it becomes our economy becomes a driver for all the other nations with whom we cooperate. And hence, all our engagements in the Indian Ocean Region and all our engagements in the Pacific Region are very important to us from the foreign policy that we are pursuing. The question that comes up is, how does it impact the security issues that we deal with? Any engagement that takes place, be it commercial, be it trade, be it for any other matter, always has a underpinning of security concerns with whom so ever you engage. And therefore, when we look at today's topic, where we are looking at the dynamics of and the challenges of the security in this region, it is quite clear that India is well poised, is well placed to pursue these with the Indo Pacific region in a manner in which it would help us.

Lot of times when we talk of Indo Pacific region, a question always comes up what is India doing with South China Sea? Some people call it South China Sea; some people call it East Vietnam Sea; some people call it differently at various times; India has been very consistent; very clear in enunciating its policy that the UN Convention on Law of Seas has to be followed by all nations in the international spirit in which it was worked up. And it is being advocating that the freedom of navigation in this area is a must, in consistent with the policy that the international organizations have laid down, that freedom of navigation must be permitted and no nation should unnecessary obstruct that freedom of navigation, And you would find that it is this consistency in our policy that has always been advocated in all the fora's and all the meetings and all the various international arenas wherever this issue is discussed; where we always come out with this particular line. We feel that any engagement in the Indo Pacific region, both in Indian Ocean as well as in Pacific Ocean, is in the interest in ensuring that there is freedom of trade and commerce; there is freedom of ensuring that whatever passes through this area can go through without being obstructed by others.

We also look at this area not becoming an arena where terrorism can come up. This is an important segment of non-conventional threats that which we face, we are looking at piracy not showing its head into this area and as most of you would be aware, we have seen piracy both, in the Indian ocean and beyond as well as we have seen piracy in certain areas towards our East. We want to ensure that there is freedom permitted to the vessels that pass through. Both, which are of commerce and which are warships going from one country to another. There is an active engagement pursued by our navy in our neighbourhood. All this is meant to strengthen our ties in both trade and commerce, economic and security areas. Our concerns remain that if we do not do this then, we are leaving the area open in which there will be people to exploit the various nations that exist out here and it may ultimately prove detrimental to a nation which has got almost 7500 kms of coastline. History tells us that it is always been this coastline which is proved vulnerable to us and earlier we look at it seriously, the better it would be for us if we have to address the security concerns that we face.

Act East Policy

There are many things that come up when we look into the policy of 'Act East'. You are aware of when we talk of geographic connectivity; the 'Kaladan' project is proceeding well. It was going slowly earlier. We feel that with the 70 to 80 percent of the work completed on the port and money sanctioned for the road infrastructure, it would be another two to three years that the 'Kaladan' project would be fully operational. We are looking at the road connectivity through Myanmar to Thailand. In this, one phase of sanctioning of various bridges that would come up has been sanctioned. The road work is already in the pipeline in terms of sanctioning and I am sure that this connectivity along with what we have between our North East and Bangladesh would allow for the connectivity with ASEAN as well as our own neighbourhood. Along with this, remains the main concern of ensuring that our North East develops in a manner that it is able to take advantages of this connectivity because if you do not create the backend connectivity into the North East region of ours then it is of no use where trade and commerce are concerned. That is being looked at seriously so that we can develop our own North East in the best possible manner where, it becomes an area which is useful for trade and commerce with our neighbourhood on both, East and West where the North East is concerned. Now with all these connectivity and all the engagements that are taking place, the most important issue is what do we see in the future? As we do crystal gazing we find that this 'Act East' policy of our would strengthen the architecture that is being looked at in terms of better connectivity of people, better connectivity in terms of how we exploit the religious links that we have, better connectivity in terms of the exchanges of academia as well as institutions with our own country which ensures that there is better understanding between people and lastly, it ensures that there is better understanding of the security concerns of each country in this region with India. And, that is what will help in ensuring that the dynamics of the challenges that we face in this region are well addressed for the future as the time goes by.

Conclusion

Each nation towards our east has its own concerns. Each nation has its own concern in terms of security, each nation has its own concern in terms of threat, that it feels and each nation seeks a friend which would be able to assist them in understanding these threats and helping them when the time comes. Now how this help will materialize is a matter that can be sorted by the experts much later, but what is important is the base has to be laid down. And that is the base that is being worked at, as part of our foreign policy. I seriously feel that the type of discussions you would have, you would be able to dissect various issues that are involved and come up with certain recommendations that would help the policy planners as well as the foreign policy that India follows in terms of understanding the security dynamics as well as understanding what is it that you all look at which would help us in further honing our own engagement with the countries in our neighbourhood. I rest my case here by saying that we understand the importance of Indo Pacific region, we understand that more engagement has to be done but as you would realise, foreign policy of any nation does not move very fast. It has to be slow, it has to be steady, it has to ensure that nobody feels that too much of pushing is being done but they come together willingly because they have common interests and common concerns. I am sure we are on right path at the moment and we are looking at this issue in a very pragmatic manner. With this thank you very much. If you have any question subsequently, I will be very glad to answer that.

PART - I

The Indo-Pacific as a Geo-strategic Concept and Construct

Strategic & Geostrategic Context

Vice Admiral AG Thapliyal, AVSM & Bar (Retd)

The term **'Indo - Pacific'** in the geostrategic and geo-economic sense is a recently coined one from the earlier often used 'Asia - Pacific' that was used to define most of the region connecting the nations in the Indian Ocean Region(IOR) and the Western Pacific through the Southeast Asia region. In fact, the term has been coined to highlight the strategic and geopolitical importance of the region where security, economic and territorial issues have a preponderant maritime flavour underscoring the importance of the oceans and the seas in the nature of connectivity. Over a period of time differing definitions have been attempted to delineate the geographic boundaries of the Indo-Pacific region. The common factor binding the littorals together has been their dependence on sea-borne trade for their well being and even existence.

Further, Asia as a continent was divided by the UN Statistical Division into six sub-divisions, namely North Asia, East Asia, South East Asia, South Asia, West Asia and Central Asia. The grouping of nations and various other Organisations/ Forums were also created keeping these geographical boundaries in mind such as APEC, ASEAN, SAARC, IOR-ARC etc.

The term 'Indo-Pacific' is being used increasingly in the global strategic/ geo-political discourse, though as per Wikipedia the term was first used in a January 2007 article in the *IDSA Journal 'Strategic Analysis'* titled "*Security of Sea Lines: Prospects for India-Japan Cooperation*" authored by Gurpreet Khurana. In the article, the term 'Indo-Pacific' refers to the maritime space stretching from the littorals of East Africa and West Asia, across the Indian Ocean and Western Pacific Ocean, to the littorals of East Asia.

The spirit of the term was picked up by Japan's Prime Minister Shinzo Abe, as reflected in his speech to the Indian Parliament in August 2007 that talked about the *"Confluence of the Indian and Pacific Oceans"* as *"the dynamic coupling as seas of freedom and of prosperity"* in the *"broader Asia"*. From about 2011 onwards, the term has been used frequently by strategic analysts and high-level government/military leadership in Australia, Japan and the US to denote the said region. However, a formal/official documented articulation of the term first appeared in Australia's Defence White Paper, 2013. It has been argued that the concept of the Indo-Pacific may lead to a change in popular "mental maps" of how the world is understood in strategic terms.

The vast Indian Ocean and Western Pacific are drawn together by natural resource flows, globalized supply chains, and international distribution networks. The waters of the Indo-Pacific region represent an increasingly critical arena for maritime geopolitics, security, trade, and environmental policy action—issues that have transformed the region into a major crossroads of international relations. For centuries, the islands and mainland of the Indo-Pacific were simply features of the Indian Ocean thoroughfare. Today, increasing flows of commerce, investment, and people are linking the Indian Ocean and Pacific nations together and to the rest of the world as part of an emerging global trading network.

The region has its mix trend towards integration/cooperation and competition. On one hand forums like the ARF, IORA, ADMM Plus and EAS aim towards building cooperation which send a strong signal towards regional stability, on the other hand lie historical territorial disputes, especially in the maritime domain and regional flashpoints, which increase the risk of conflict and competition. Thus, the interplay of overlapping and intersecting interests in the region presents a complex strategic environment characterized by growth and integration as well as potential for destabilising the region and increasing the vulnerability due to greater interdependence.

The Indo-Pacific is still emerging as a system which is predominantly maritime with Southeast Asia as its centre. Given its diversity and broad sweep, its security architecture is a series of sub-regions and arrangements rather than a unitary whole. It is, however, appreciated that over the next decade, the security environment around most nations of the region will be significantly influenced by how the Indo-Pacific and its architecture evolve.

The Indo-Pacific Region in the pre-colonial period - Linkages and Connectivity between Regions

Trade is as old as the beginning of settled urban life. Though ordinary needs were met by local agriculture and local manufacturing, the earliest cities had specific requirements that could not be satisfied locally. The formation of an intensive trading network spanning the whole Asia-Pacific region became possible only after the rise of empires which could provide peace and security, build roads and ports and maintain them. In the East, the expansion of Han China under Wu-ti by the close of the first century (140-87 BC) created an economic block of vast dimension. It possessed an elaborate network of roads and a highly organised system of transport and marketing, which encouraged regional participations and an unprecedented interchange of goods and manufactured products.

The trade did not halt at the frontier. Chinese, Indian and Arab rulers sent missions to various part of the neighbourhood, often through sea routes. Shortly after 128 BC the famous Silk Route came into operation.It started at *Tunhwang* on China's far Western boundary, and skirted North or South of the *Takla Makan* Desert to *Kashgar*, before crossing the *Pamirs* and debouching into *Bactria, Persia* and the *Mediterranean* coastal belt. But the Silk Route, spectacular though it was, was less important in economic terms than the sea route to India and the Far East and the traffic along which increased greatly after the discovery of the 'Monsoon' around 100 BC. Prior to this discovery, the coastal traffic, had been mainly in Arab and Indian hands. Now upto 120 Greek vessels a year, some with a carrying capacity of 500 tons plied direct to the Indian ports of *Barbaricum, Barygaza* (Broach) and *Muziris* (Kochi), where they picked up Eastern cargoes shipped by

Indian merchants from *Go Oc Eo* in Southern Cambodia and carried them to *Berenice* and other Red Sea ports for transport on to *Alexandria* and thence to other parts of the Roman empire.

While these far-flung trading links have been impressive to say the least, their economic importance remains questionable during the period. It is interesting to note that during the same period as the Han empire, Rome was also trying to develop cultural and trade links with the outside world. While both empires were self sufficient in essential commodities, it is surmised that foreign trade was essentially a luxury trade, marginal to every day needs. On the other hand, there is no doubt that foreign trade contributed directly to cultural interchange and spread of great world religions. On the flip side, the less happy consequences was the spread of disease and pestilence. Earlier the armies were blamed for transmitting the epidemics, but now even the caravans and merchant shipping were held responsible for the same. The devastating effects of such epidemic on vulnerable populations can well be understood, since only "One or Two out of Hundred survived". The sharp fall in the able-bodied manpower caused by imported pestilences also affected the capacities of these empires to withstand the barbarian onslaught in the 4th and 5th centuries.

The revival of Islam after 1300 and the great wave of Muslim expansion that followed, dominated the next four centuries, far more so than European expansion which had only marginal effects till 1700. By 1630, the three Muslim empires controlled a wide belt of territory from the frontiers of Austria and Morocco to the borders of China, the foothills of Himalayas and the Bay of Bengal. But in the changing world Islam remained static. All three Muslim empires were essentially land based; but now hegemony was passing to the sea, and to the peoples on the fringe - the Dutch, the French, the English - who knew how to master and exploit the seas.

Military and political reverses did not impede the expansion of Chinese culture and political institutions to all her neighbouring states. Korea, Japan and Southeast Asia were the most affected, though by then Southeast Asia had come in contact with Indian (from about 1300 AD) and Islamic influences. In Southeast Asia the small temple states of the ninth to twelfth centuries like Prambanan, Angkor, Pagan established under Hindu and Buddhist influence, gave way after the 13th century to new political centres like Phnom Penh, Pegu while in Vietnam, where Chinese attempts to re-conquest failed, and a new kingdom of Dai Viet arose. The formative influence and assimilation of Hinduism, Buddhism and Confucianism defined the distinctive character of the Southeast Asian civilisation.

Spices were staple intercontinental trade in this period and was considered indispensable, easy to handle and highly profitable. Both Europe and China were dependent for supplies on the spice producing regions of Asia, particularly the *Moluccas and the Malay archipelago*. The resultant transactions, which stretched from the Red Sea and Persian Gulf to the South China Sea were largely in the hands of Arabs and Indian middlemen, finally hinging on the port city of Malacca. Between 1405 and 1433 AD, the Chinese under the Ming dynasty, sent seven expeditions under Admiral Zheng. He through the Strait of Malacca to the Indian Ocean and beyond, but this enterprise ceased abruptly after 1440.

Impact of the colonial period on these linkages and connectivity till the Cold War

Meanwhile Portugal which was probing down the West coast of Africa in search of gold, got financial backing from Genoa for its venture to search for an alternative route to the East, to cut out Genoa's rival Venice. This was the time, when Constantinople had fallen in 1453, and Genoa had lost its eastern markets. When the Portuguese reached India in 1498, and Columbus, despatched by Portugal's rival Spain, reached America, a new era had begun.

Once in the Indian Ocean, the Portuguese reached their goal; Malabar in 1498, Malacca in 1511 and Moluccas in 1512. The English, French and Dutch were unwilling to abandon the profitable trade with South and Southeast Asia to the Portuguese and Spaniards and the later years of the 16th and first half of the 17th century saw a determined and ultimately successful effort to breach their privileged position. After 1500, direct sea contact was established between continents and regions, and while the progress was slow, by the time of the death of the last great explorer James Cook, in 1779, the worldwide network of relationships had been formed which characterises the modern era and differentiated it from all preceding times. The thousand year old pattern, centred around the Mediterranean, gave way to an Atlantic economy, and the whole economic and political balance in Europe shifted dramatically.

When Albuquerque conquered Malacca for the king of Portugal in 1511, the famous empires of Srivijaya and Majapahit had disappeared. The Portuguese dominated the spice trade through a chain of fortified trading stations, linked by naval power. Their trading monopoly was challenged after the arrival of the Dutch and the British. The Dutch began a systematic conquest of the Portuguese settlements, capturing Malacca in 1641, and gradually extended control over Java, expelling the British from *Bantam (near Jakarta)* in 1682.

In India, the British Empire sustained through sea power till 1947, enabled the English East India Company to checkmate the ambitions of the able French Governor Joseph Dupleix, to expand French influence in South India. However, between 1815 and 1914, under the impact of the Industrial Revolution, the character of European imperialism changed. Earlier, the motivating force has been the search for the riches of the Orient, with the stakes confined to 'Trading stations' and 'Strategic outposts' necessary to protect the trade. But, in the 19th century, two new factors came into play. The first, search for raw materials came around 1880, with the new phase of the Industrial revolution, without which the industry, in its new form, could not exist and the second, was the opening of the world - Turkey and Egypt in 1838, Persia in 1841, China in 1842 and even Japan in 1858 - to European, particularly British commerce. So began the scramble for natural resources, providing new impetus for colonial expansion. Between 1880 and 1914, Europe added over 8 1/2 million square miles, or one fifth of the land area of the globe, to its overseas colonial possessions.

The French conquered Indo-China in 1859 and Britain established strategic foothold in Mauritius and Seychelles. Fearing French challenge, Britain claimed sovereignty over Australia and New Zealand and consolidated its power in India besides acquiring Singapore (1819), Malacca (1824), Hong Kong (1842) and Lower Burma (1852). After 1880, the Germans and Italians also challenged the imperial powers but achieved little in this region. France gained Madagascar and some islands in the Pacific while Britain secured control over areas in the Pacific including Fiji and parts of Borneo and New Guinea. The keystone of British Empire was India, and its acquisitions were made with a view to not only bolster British control over its access to India and the Indian Ocean via the Suez Canal and East Africa, but also via Singapore and the South Pacific. It was believed that as long as it was assured of control of the Indian Ocean, the British imperial power was secure.

Equally important were the expansion of world shipping and the replacement of sailing ships by ocean-going steamships of large capacity. World trade got a further fillip with the opening of the Suez Canal in 1869 and the Panama Canal in 1914. India and China had begun to develop their own industries, but with the exception of Japan, these were small enclaves in the vast rural population. The income produced by manufacturing, benefitted the foreign investors but the bulk of the population benefitted only marginally, and per capita income in most countries seem, actually to have declined.

In China, the Ch'ing or the Manchu dynasty that had ruled from 1644 to 1911 created the world's largest and most populous empire. Later, the Chinese attempts to halt the illicit opium trade were decisively defeated by the British in the Opium war of 1839-42. The result forced the Chinese to dole out trade concessions to the European powers as also occupation of its territory by the British, French, Russians and the Japanese from 1856 to 1898. The Chinese imperial government was thoroughly discredited after the Army mutiny and fell in 1911, almost without fighting.

The Chinese Republic was proclaimed in 1912, and Sun Yat-sen as its first President was displaced within weeks by General Yuan Shih-k'ai, of the old regime. Yuan's death in 1916, involvement of the armies of provincial warlords, expansionist policies of Japan and the interfering presence of foreign powers under the Treaty of Ports continued to add to the chaos of the struggling Chinese economy. When the Paris Peace Conference in 1919 refused to abrogate Japanese and other foreign privileges, there was a massive upsurge of Chinese nationalism, finding vent in the 04th May 1919 Movement, and the starting point of the Chinese revolution.

For the next 30 years, the two main parties, the Nationalist Kuomintang Part or KMT and the Chinese Communist Party or CCP (formed in 1921) struggled to regain power, trying all possible options including elimination of warlords, mobilising uprisings, massacres and intrigue. During the Long March to Yenan in 1934-35, CCP leader Mao Tse-tung could gather widespread support by his reform programmes and post Japanese defeat in 1945, once the negotiations for a political settlement between the KMT and CCP broke down, the open civil war broke out in 1947. The Communists defeated the Nationalists in Manchuria and took Peking in January 1949. On 01 Oct 1949, the People's Republic was proclaimed, and the Nationalists fled to Taiwan.

Japan over the 17th and 18th century, despite its growth, found international recognition of Japan's new status slow to come. Concessions to unequal treaties signed earlier between Japan and outside powers were lifted in 1911 as a tribute to Japan's military successes in war with China (1894-95) and the Russo-Japanese war (1904-05). After the war, with mutual understanding with Russia, Japan annexed Korea in 1910. It had embarked to create a Japanese empire on the Asian mainland and the war of 1914-18 and the Russian revolution enabled it to gain a foothold in Shantung and Manchuria. The Western pressure compelled it to withdraw, but Japan was recognised at the Peace Conference in 1919 as a major power with a permanent seat on the Council of the League of Nations.

Japan's expansionist outlook was a product of a desire to achieve economic self-sufficiency, military security and a self-imposed leadership of Eastern Asia. Beginning with overrunning Manchuria in 1931, it then set about overrunning much of China North of the Yangtze River.

With Germany's swift defeat of France and Holland in 1940, Japan, with no possibility of militarily or politically ending the Chinese war, found its ambitions widening to include the European colonial empires in Southeast Asia. These offered the raw materials and markets that would free Japan from the economic dependence upon an increasingly unfriendly United States. The likelihood of future naval inferiority due to near completion (1944-45) of USA's rearmament programme and the economic blockade imposed upon Japan after its occupation of Indo-China in 1940 prompted Japanese action. Attack on the US Pacific Fleet at Pearl Harbour in December 1940 was an attempt to forestall American military preparation and thereby buy time needed to secure and develop Southeast Asia.

Japan surrendered in August 1945, when the US atomic bomb was dropped on Hiroshima and Nagasaki and the Soviet offensive in Manchuria was at its peak.

Retreat from Empire - after 1947

None of the European powers surrendered its colonies voluntarily. France fought stubbornly to maintain control of Indo-China, Netherlands struggled to contain the nationalists in Java who had proclaimed an Indonesian republic in 1945. Neither was successful. France too gave way after the Vietnamese victory at Dien Bien Phu in 1954. British too, had no intention of abdicating their imperial position, but continued civil disobedience and unrest forced them to create India and Pakistan in Aug 1947, followed by Burma and Ceylon. Nevertheless, Britain still clung to its base at Singapore till 1965. Britain abandoned its presence East of Suez only after 1967, when Aden was evacuated. Hong Kong was retained till 1997, and its economic success being of great benefit to China.

A large number of colonies got their independence between the periods 1960- 1980 by which time the formal structures of European imperialism had been dismantled. Namibia won independence in 1990 and 'Apartheid' was abandoned in South Africa in 1993.

Asia after Independence

The history of Asia and Africa since independence is one of constant instability. Three factors stand out: first, the seizure of power by military leaders (Egypt 1952, Pakistan 1958, Ghana 1966, Indonesia 1967), with the aim of abolishing corruption and stabilising the economy; second, the resurgence of long standing regional, tribal and religious conflicts (Naga unrest in India, Kurdish revolt in Northern Iraq, Turkey and Iran, nationalist uprisings among the Kachins, Mons, Shans and other hill peoples in Thailand and Burma); and third the persistent intervention by the great powers, especially in the Middle East. (eg Sino-Soviet rivalry behind Vietnamese invasion of Cambodia and Chinese invasion of Vietnam in 1979 and many other examples in Africa).

The Cold War from 1947

The USA and USSR emerged as the two 'Super-Powers' once the war was over. Starting as a conflict over Central Europe and divided Germany, the Cold War soon developed into a global confrontation. The USA and Soviet Union left no stone unturned to establish their respective zones of influence and proxies the world over. With the success of Communists in the Chinese civil war in Oct 1949 and the installation of a Communist regime in North Korea in 1948, the Communist insurgencies bubbled up in Vietnam, Malaya and Indonesia. The first serious conflict of the Cold war was fought in Korea, when North Korea tried to bring the south into the Communist bloc by force. Seeing it as a world-wide Communist conspiracy the American policy hereafter, was to 'contain' the Communist power by a series of encircling alliances. NATO was followed by SEATO in 1954 and the Baghdad Pact was converted into CENTO in 1959.

While the USA committed some 543,000 ground troops by 1968, as also the naval and air forces, it failed to defeat the guerrilla tactics of the Vietnamese National Liberation Front and in 1973, with the US economy under severe pressure, President Nixon called a halt. Soviet invasion of Afghanistan in 1979 fuelled another round of confrontation between the superpowers.

The Cold war kept the region fragmented and saw the emergence of various initiatives by countries in the region so as to have a collective voice in managing the affairs that directly impacted their growth and well being. The region witnessed creation of alliances and groupings which indicated their allegiance to a specific bloc. Thus, over the past six decades efforts have been underway by the countries of the region, and many with reasonable success, to establish cooperative and collaborative mechanisms which would not only address the economic development of the region but also factor in the myriad of security and stability issues that have dogged the nations of this Region.

A new era of cooperation began under Reagan and Gorbachev which led to the reduction of nuclear arsenals, and Soviet withdrawal from Afghanistan and East Europe and joint agreement on a reunification of Germany in 1990, brought the classic Cold War to an end.

The Indo-Pacific as a Security Construct

Rear Admiral K Raja Menon (Retd)

The previous speaker has gone into the historical aspect of how the Indo-Pacific term was coined and the expressions came about, and have therefore laid the groundwork for me to continue from there. Certainly among the Indian maritime thinkers I would like to add my credits to Capt Gurpreet Khurana who used the expression in his writing as early as 2007. Normally the security construct comes after the geo-political foundations have been laid. In this case, I think the American perhaps unwittingly laid down the security construct, perhaps in a fit of absent-mindedness – because look at the cold war and post-cold war geographical limits of the Pacific command.

As you can see the western boundary of PACOM runs along he Indo-Pakistan border thereby leaving the entire Indian Ocean, South East Asia, the Malacca Straits and the Bay of Bengal in the jurisdiction of the Pacific command from Honolulu. The first positive indications of this was the visit of the PACOM Cdr Admiral Chuck Larson to NHQ in 1992 where he gave a briefing in the Naval war room and made us aware that somebody in Honolulu was interested in the Arabian Sea and the Bay of Bengal. We still didn't take it all that seriously until the intellectual connection between Honolulu and New Delhi began to build up in the next decade. There was constant interaction between the naval staffs and between the East – West center and the APCSS and Indian think tanks – I remember making quite a few trips to Honolulu in the late 1990s and early 2000s.

Perhaps it was after 9/11 and the entry of the US Navy to support the operation in Afghanistan, and the movement of the Taliban from Afghanistan to Pakistan, that things became more focused. We had a lot of problems with Pakistan including the 2002 standoff, but our compliments to the Americans, locally and in the Gulf, was met with the reply that we should deal with Honolulu. I think it was then that we began to truly understand the importance of PACOM. Certainly when PACOM's boundaries were first set up I don't think the US was thinking seriously about linking the Indian Ocean with the Pacific. The American focus was solely on the West Pacific and North-East Asia so the neglect was mutual until the geo-politics began to permanently change. And for this we primarily have to look at the blistering pace of the rise of China when it was clocking close to 10 percent GDP growth and devouring the world's resources. Of course, a major part of these resources were coming from the last untapped area of the world – Africa and all the resources from Africa would have to transit the Indian Ocean.

Figure 1: China-Africa trade to keep growing
USD bn

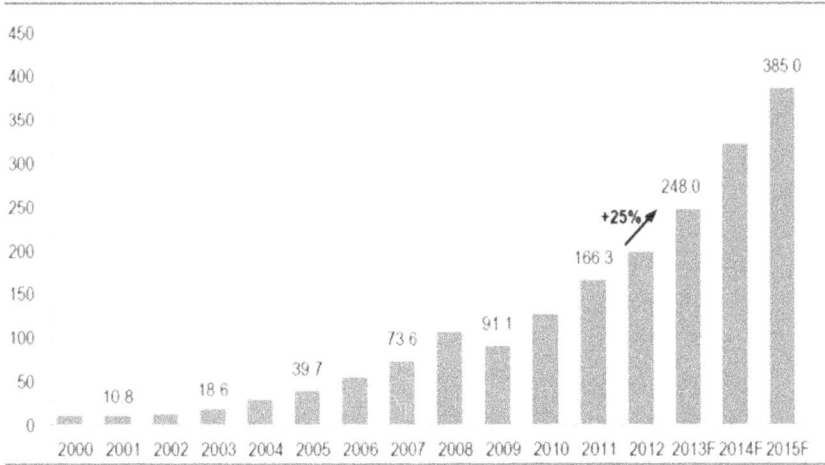

Sources: MOFCOM, Standard Chartered Research

If you see the projected growth of Africa-China trade on the graph you will get an idea of what implication there are for Chinese SLOCs in the Indian Ocean.

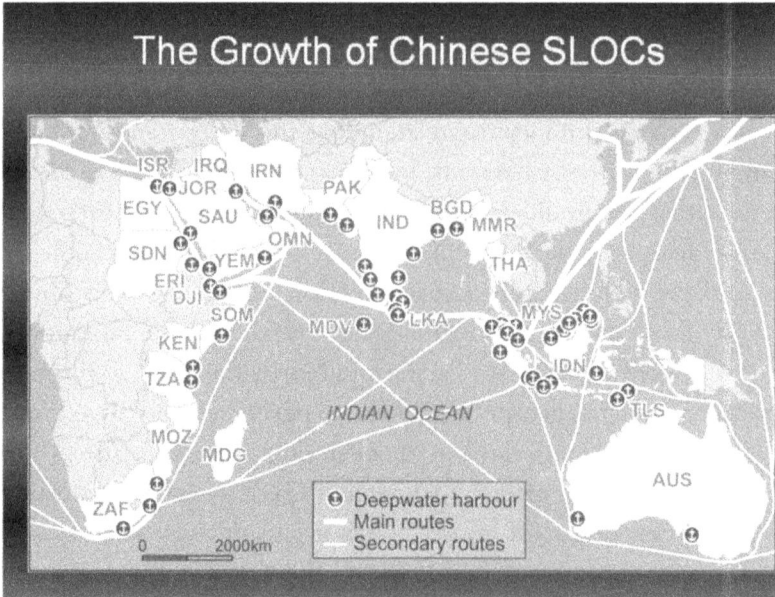

The huge growth of China's SLOCs in the Indian Ocean makes it imperative that Beijing takes a call on their security. It has three options:

a. Cooperate with the international system in preserving the safety of its SLOCs

b. Outsource the security through bilateral alliances or understandings with the US or India.

c. Make a serious foray into the Indian Ocean with the PLAN.

Chinese literature would seem to indicate that it prefers the last option – to operate the PLAN in the Indian Ocean at some time in the future, when the logistic chain has been tied up. The Cdr of the PLAN's East Seas fleet in 2012 made the statement on the freedom and safety of the Indian Ocean sea lanes, although he said that this would be accomplished through security cooperation with other navies – we haven't seen any evidence of such cooperation so far. In June 2013 the Blue Book of the Chinese Academy of Social Sciences (CASS) had a chapter on India's look East Policy and it stated that a US-India axis was building in the Indian Ocean. It went on to say that so far China followed a 'moderate' policy in the Indian Ocean but the changing dynamics created by Japan, Australia, India and the US would force China into a more 'proactive' role.

Chinese academicians close to the party have put out articles stating the Indo-Pacific is a US construct deliberately made so as to obtain hegemony in the Indian Ocean and control the choke points (US Indian Ocean strategy, Pacific Journal, June 2013 Sum Xinpu, Kurming). Chinese analysts have commented on the launching of India's aircraft carrier Vikrant and stated that India wishes to dominate the Indian Ocean and exert a greatest presence in the Pacific Ocean. They allege that the US pushes India to integrate into the US system, but India so far has maintained an independent position. (FU Xiapiang, CICIR, China Daily, 12 Aug 2013). The article went on to say that although conflict is predicted between US, China and India, these countries have different strategic goals and only India wishes to use its geographic position to attempt to dominate the Indian Ocean, all by itself.

Robert Kaplan surmises that considering China's difficulty in maintaining a constant presence in the Indian ocean, but because of the conflicting strategic imperative of protecting the energy routes through the Indian ocean, Beijing will be pragmatic and follow a 'harmonious seas' approach and push for a constructive engagement with the US

The Maritime Silk Road

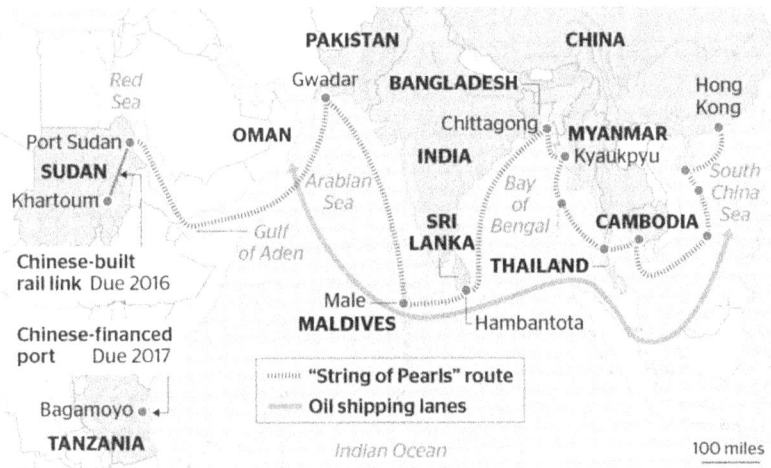

and Indian navies. In the meanwhile it will work economically to woo the Indian Ocean littorals away from US influence to prevent the US from crafting an anti-China alliance in the Indian Ocean.

The question for us is whether this is the strategic rationale behind the Maritime Silk Road? There are many in India who have stated that they do not see the defining parameters of the Maritime Silk road – but there is a theory I would like to advance. China, according to Kaplan firmly believes that India will preserve its strategic autonomy despite US presence. China would like to accommodate India's position by its 'look west' policy. But as far as the other littoral powers are concerned it would like to use its financial clout and economic prowess to keep them from banding together against Beijing. This factor combined with other factors such as being excluded from the TPP, the US opposition to the Asian infrastructure investment bank and others have resulted in the strategy of the Maritime Silk Road where China crafts some kind of an economic alliance. How else can China use its surplus cash for a strategic objective with long term consequences that are beneficial to Beijing?

Harsh Pant, an Indian scholar thinks differently and posits an India-China rivalry. He quotes Shen Dingli that China is entitled to foreign bases like all other powers, however the string of pearls theory that he bases his arguments on has been partly discredited, except for Gwadar. Pant also believes that for China to dominate the Indian Ocean is not possible in the near future, but Gwadar could be a serious challenge to India, even if at present it only has commercial application. So my view is that in the long term there will undoubtedly be a PLAN presence in the Indian Ocean, but the Chinese will spend a decade or more preparing for that presence by setting up the supply chain in the form of dual use bases founded on the Maritime Silk Road. I don't think that this stops us from joining the MSR in any way. We should join if it is going to help us build our infrastructure with help from Chinese investment. The adverse consequences will come a decade or two later and we can face it at that stage with a stronger navy.

As far as the West Pacific and South China seas are concerned, we, in India do not have the economic or naval heft to operate there in a substantial way. True, we have drilling blocs off Vietnam and our navy must have the freedom to cooperate with the South-East Asian navies, particularly Vietnam.

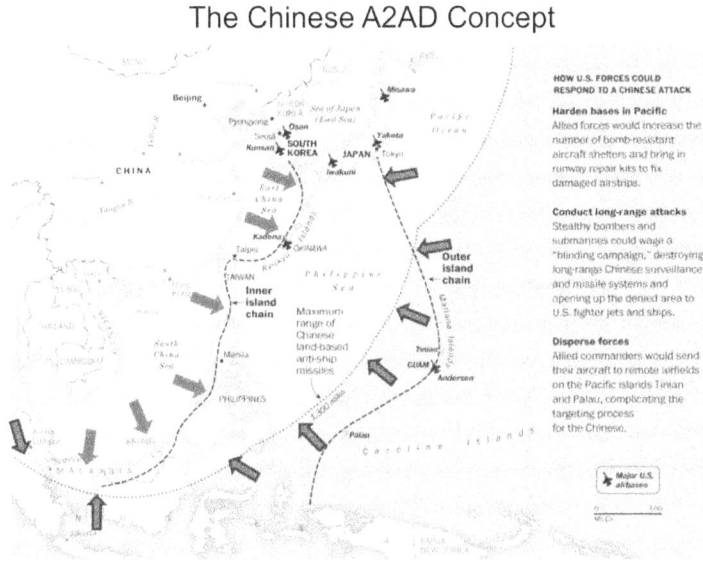

The Chinese A2AD Concept

But the tactical situation in the West Pacific will be eventually decided between the Chinese Anti-Access Area-Denial (A2AD) concept, to deny the US navy an approach to the Taiwan Straits, and the US air sea battle concept, which attempts to neutralize the Chinese A2AD idea. The PLAN will always be hesitant to exit the West Pacific and operate in the Indian Ocean as long as it is tied down to the West Pacific. In other words, the Indians have a stake in the outcome of the West Pacific coastal competition between the US and China. In my opinion this outcome can become favourable for China only if it maintains a high economic growth rate for another two or three decades and seriously overtakes the US as an economic and military power. At present the innovative developments going on in the US, in the form of large lasers, the hyper plane and the rail gun will probably preserve US military superiority for another few decades in the Pacific.

No one foresees an actual conflict between the US and China despite the tension in the South China Seas but all countries would like to know whose geo-political position is a greater success and choose their options accordingly. So the competition between the US and China for maritime supremacy in the West Pacific is real, although the US has gone to great pains to explain that its pivot to the East is to engage China and reflect the reality of a growing China and a PLAN.

Eventually Chinese literature is insistent that it has a Malacca Dilemma. This idea has grown entirely and autonomously in Beijing without any other country suggesting that China has a choke point problem in the Malacca Straits. Beijing has made many efforts to build direct pipelines from the Indian Ocean, but nevertheless the larger part of oil for China will come across the Indian Ocean through the Straits of Malacca to the South China Seas. If I was a naval planner in Beijing, this fact would cause me anxiety and there is no way that I would accept that the PLAN has no right to operate freely in the Indian Ocean.

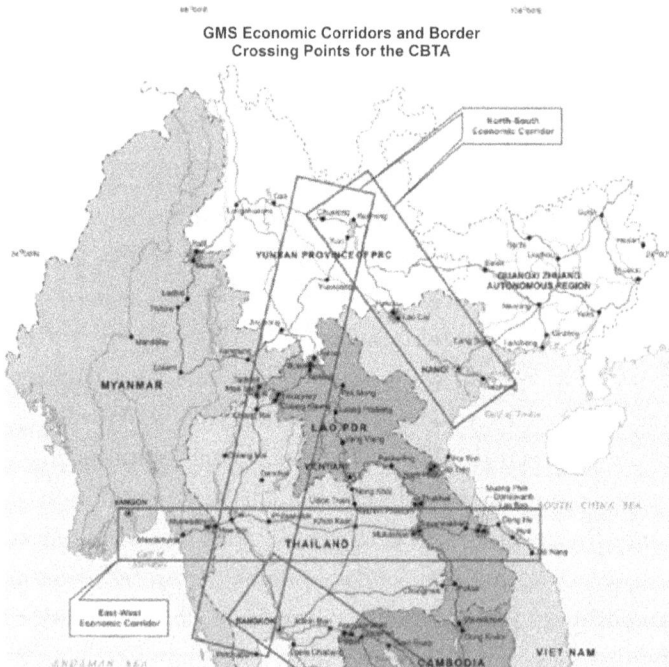

So the geographical barriers of the South-East Asian land mass cannot any more separate the Indian and Pacific Ocean, particularly because continental connectivity is shortening distances all over the world. The South-East Asian rail and road connectivity and telecommunications directly make the land mass virtually disappear and give a seamless connectivity to the Indian and Pacific Oceans.

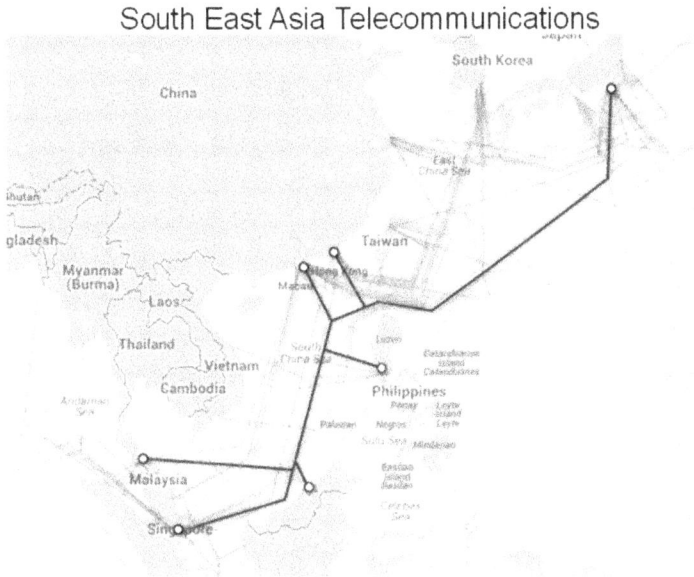

South East Asia Telecommunications

The interconnectivity has been evidenced by the Malabar exercises where maritime nations across the Indo-Pacific, Japan, the US, Australian and Japan navies join regularly in maritime exercises. Today it doesn't matter who began the security competition to create the Indo-Pacific concept, but both the US and China seem committed to it, the US with the boundaries of PACOM including both oceans and China by launching a Maritime Silk Road, in pursuit of its plan to operate in the Indian ocean.

The International Implications of the Maritime Silk Road: A view from Russia

Ambassador Gleb A Ivashentsov

The 21st century has given a head start to global political and economic changes, putting an end to some political projects and opening up opportunities for others. The centre of gravity of the world politics is shifting today from the Atlantic and the West to Eurasia and the East. Today, the single Eurasian space — China with South-East Asia, Russia with the Eurasian Union, plus India, the Middle East and Africa, are also becoming increasingly Eurasia-oriented. This is pressing the economy of the previously omnipotent trio of the United States, Europe and Japan. Although, the outlines of 'Greater Eurasia' are still vague and, in many ways, unclear, one cannot fail to see the objective and long-term nature of the processes involved in emergence of a new transnational economic and political structure. The United States is fiercely resisting these developments. It is broadening efforts to revive the united consolidated West as it used to be in the Cold War time. It is renovating and strengthening the NATO supporting it with military alliances in the Asia-Pacific, but special stress is being laid on forming two mighty economic blocs under the US command viz. the Trans-Pacific and Trans-Atlantic partnerships.

The US actions are a convincing proof of the correctness of Lenin's words that politics is the most concentrated expression of economics. Any time when a potential competitor to the US global economic domination appears on the scene, Washington takes steps to limit that competitor's abilities, first by the economic diplomacy measures, and if these measures don't succeed, by political and even military pressure.

For instance, when the European Union came up as an influential economic actor, the US tried their best to found the APEC in 1989 so that to confront the economic advance of Greater Europe in interaction with fast growing East Asian economies. But as China had strengthened its positions in the APEC space, the US in 2011came up with the initiative of the Trans-Pacific Partnership to which neither China, nor Russia were invited. While announcing on October 5th at Atlanta the formation of the TPP, President Obama unequivocally proclaimed: "We can't let countries like China write the rules of the global economy. We should write those rules" (chinadaily.com.cn›…2015-10/09/content_22136461.htm)

The US-China confrontation

Some people draw parallels between the present U.S.—China rivalry and the Soviet-American antagonism of the Cold War. However, there is a dramatic difference. The Soviet-American stand-off was rigorously ideological on both sides—not just competition between two superpowers but a confrontation of two systems, with peaceful coexistence seen both by Moscow and Washington as *a lull before a decisive battle.*

In Chinese terminology, relations between China and America have developed into a *competitive interaction*, with the United States economically dependent on China to a greater extent than on any of its allies. Since China is in the ascendant within the existing global architecture, it is not interested in breaking down the arrangement. China intends to reformat the arrangement to serve its own needs.

However, Washington is not willing to give up the conductor's place in the Indo-Pacific or global *concert of nations*. As China's strength is based on its trade and economic advancement, the U.S *'Pivot To Asia'* is primarily intended to create a real danger to sea routes used by China for 90 percent of its foreign trade. The focus being on the military buildup in the Indo-Pacific, stronger ties with allies and bridge-building with new partners. And all this is definitely against Beijing, as the United States is aggressively interfering in Chinese territorial disputes with ASEAN states in the South China Sea and placing China as the opposing number in its Transpacific Partnership.

China has responded with the concepts of the Silk Road Economic Belt and the 21st Century Maritime Silk Route. That is reasonable. The Washington-led system of alliances is aimed to impede China's advancement to the Pacific and to the eastward in general. But the path to the westward is free from the US interference, promising China with the access to raw materials and markets as well as to the growing general influence in the continental Asia.

The Eurasia underbelly

The 21st Century Maritime Silk Route lies in the Indian and Pacific oceans touching the lands which may be viewed as the Eurasia underbelly. Currently, this is a highly turbulent area, where globalization processes combine with leadership struggle and arms race, rising affluence alongside deepening poverty, and financial tensions and territorial disputes are prevalent. The Indo-Pacific may boast the world's busiest trade route covering 70 percent global oil and 50 percent global container shipments. http://www.perspektivy.info/print.php?ID=104809) And then there are Afghanistan and Iraq, whose territories are mired in protracted military conflicts, Yemen — which is joining their number, as well as the offensive of the so-called Islamic State.

As for Russia, its interest to the developments in the Indian Ocean area is quite natural. First, the Indian Ocean historically has had a great transit importance, for it is connecting its Black Sea ports with those in the Russian Far East, and hence the safety of the SLOC passing via the region is important. Secondly, it was no secret that the growth of the US military presence in the Indian Ocean from early 1970s was initially to a large extent directed at creating a strategic threat to the Soviet Union from south.

Twenty years ago Zbigniew Brzezinski wrote that "America's global primacy is directly dependent on how long and how effectively its preponderance on the Eurasian continent is sustained," although he viewed this condition as "temporary" (www.takeoverworld.info/Grand_ Chessboard.pdf. p.30) The American geopolitical guru's prediction about United States' loss of dominance in Eurasia seems to be coming true. Despite its huge political, economic and military power, the United States accounts for only three percent of the global population and will not be able to amalgamate the diverse Eurasian components into a uniform American standard.

Two factors have significantly limited the US capacities in the Eurasia underbelly this year. First, it is the developments around Iran. The adoption of the Joint Comprehensive Plan of Action on Iran's nuclear program is to unlock Iran's active participation in the regional political and economic affairs in its own right. As Iran is practically the only "Greater Middle East" country constantly increasing its economic, scientific, technological and defence potential, owning 10 percent global petroleum and 16 percent global natural gas deposits, with the GDP over that of Egypt, a literate and relatively young population of 80 Million and a highly educated elite, there is little doubt that it could become a new "Asian Tiger" in a comparatively near future. No doubt that this tiger will walk by himself not seeking guidance from American trainers.

Second, India and Pakistan have joint the Shanghai Cooperation Organisation (the SCO). India's foreign trade no less than that of China depends on the safety of the Indian Ocean sea lanes. With India as its member along with China and Russia, and Iran free to join after the sanctions imposed on it are lifted, the SCO is progressively becoming the continental Asia' s main development and security forum and a potential link between the continental Silk Road Economic Belt and the 21st Century Maritime Silk Route.

Toward Peace and Stability via Economic Cooperation

Joint implementation of long-term economic projects is definitely the best way to improve mutual trust and reduce tensions between neighbouring states. Europe had an opportunity for the experience in late 1960s and early 1970s, when laying of pipelines from the Soviet Union to West Europe and participation of West European firms in construction of large industrial plants in the USSR effectively worked to stifle the mutual mistrust of the Cold War and open a path to political détente in Europe, peaking with the 1975 Conference on Security and Cooperation in Europe and the establishment of the OSCE. Naturally, the direct duplication of the 40-year-old European practice in the present Indo-Pacific is not appropriate, although some elements might be brought into play.

The Maritime Silk Route initiative is to be thoroughly studied in this connection. It is free of political or institutional proposals. For now, the idea is broadly mulled as the construction and development of transport infrastructure along the Maritime Silk Road to be later augmented by FTAs, coordination of customs procedures and quality standards, advancement of e-trade, etc. In fact, as far as the countries on the Indian Ocean's northern coast are concerned, these proposals largely coincide with the activities of the Asia-Pacific Economic Cooperation (APEC) forum in relation of the APEC space.

India bears great significance for Maritime Silk Road development. As the most important nation in the Indian Ocean, India is going through a fast economic growth, and can be a significant partner on the Maritime Silk Road in the fields of infrastructure, trade, finance and people-to-people exchanges.

As part of its 21st Century Maritime Silk Route initiative, Beijing has expressed disassociating itself from any kind of competition, suggesting a project that would bypass other schemes in the Eurasian periphery but could absorb them if the need arises. Unlike the United States, which relies on military and political tools to push forward its economic interests, China offers cash and political neutrality.

Finances for infrastructure

The structural deficit in finances for infrastructure in developing Asian states is the key barrier to growth in the Indo-Pacific. This is why the Chinese initiative of establishing the Asian Infrastructure Investment Bank (AIIB) was broadly welcomed. In October 2014 China signed the memorandum to establish the AIIB with only 21 Asian states, and currently over 50 countries are joining the project, including Russia, EU leading states, South Korea, Brazil, South Africa, Australia, Egypt, as well as the Gulf monarchies (http://www.vestifinance.ru/articles/55297). The only economic powers staying out are the United States and Japan. Some Westerners believe that the AIIB may effectively compete in Asia against the World Bank and the International Monetary Fund, and against the Washington and Tokyo-dominated Asian Development Bank.

For Moscow, the AIIB represents a win-win situation. Russia's economic integration into the Indo-Pacific is hardly possible in the absence of any involvement in infrastructure, first of all, energy and transport, Russia's trump cards in the Indo-Pacific space. AIIB money may go toward building gas and oil pipelines and electric power lines from Russia to adjacent countries, to the modernization of the Trans-Siberian and Baikal-Amur railways and Russian ports in the Pacific, as well as to the development of Northern Sea Route.

The creation of the International North-South Transport Corridor from the Iranian port of Bandar Abbas in the Indian Ocean via Iran, Transcaucasia and Central Asia along both Caspian coasts to Moscow and St. Petersburg in Russia and Northern Europe could prove to be of a particular value for the economic integration of Indo-Pacific countries, and for the development of their trade links with the Eurasian Economic Union and West Europe. In 2000, a relevant intergovernmental agreement was signed by Russia, Iran and India, who were later joined by Azerbaijan, Armenia, Belarus, Kazakhstan, Oman and Syria. On September 29, 2014, participants of the 4th Caspian Summit in Astrakhan also supported the idea.

The Main Issue

The struggle for Eurasia is becoming the main issue for decades to come. The point is not to isolate the United States but to replace the U.S. led Western-centric world (monitored by American banks and protected by American aircraft-carriers), with a polycentric arrangement, which would provide for the equality and respect of interests for large and small states in politics, mutual benefits in economics, compatibility and mutual enrichment of civilizations in culture, mutual trust and cooperation in the security area, and shared responsibility in global affairs.

China's Role as a Maritime Power and its Impact on Security Environment in East Asia and Indo Pacific

Dr Mumin Chen

Introduction

China's assertive actions on the Pacific Ocean and potential consequences

China's strategic objectives after 2006 were to expand its navel influence from territorial waters and contiguous zones of 24 nautical miles to exclusive economic zones (EEZs) of 250 nautical miles. By claiming the Spratly Islands as well as the entire South China Sea as territories and territorial waters, China would be able to extend its sphere of influence for another 1,500 nautical miles beyond the homeland. Such an attempt requires establishment of a blue-water carrier task group, and a naval task force capable of conducing long-distance combats. China started conducting task group-level far-sea maneuver exercises targeting at the Second Island chain in 2007, and made such exercises a constant training program after 2013. In 2014, China further integrated its naval aviation and air force into such exercises. Three related questions will be discussed here:

1. Is PLA Navy capable of fighting against the US carrier strike group?

2. How will China utilize its blue-water joint task group to respond

to possible clash with Japan over the territorial dispute in Diaoyutai/Senkaku Islands?

3. Whether we can interpret China's military buildups in the South China Sea as an attempt to building a maritime hegemon in future?

First of all, China already has a 60,000+ tons aircraft carrier, and is expected to build another 2 to 4 carriers. China also has plans for building more advanced large air-Defence destroyers, logistic and support ships, amphibious ships, and multi-function corvettes, and it seems that China is making preparations to establish its own blue-water carrier joint task groups. According to the naval guidelines designed by Admiral Liu Huaqing in 1985 as well as China's *Defence White Papers* released over past few years, China's naval strategic development still focuses on the Western Pacific, and the Second Island Chain, in particular, which also meet predictions of the United States.

However, the Chinese Navy remains incapable of fighting against the US carrier strike groups. If they want to acquire such capabilities, they have to build large nuclear-powered aircraft carriers with 100,000-tons, and carrying more than 90 aircrafts. In addition, since China's land-based air power will be hindered by US airbases located in the First Island Chain, China's aircraft carrier squadrons have to be able to fight independently. On the other hand, owning a carrier does not necessarily equal to having the long-range strike capability. Meanwhile, the Chinese carrier squadron is still developing its combat capabilities as the command and control of a carrier squadron requires full operational coordination in space, electromagnetic warfare, air, surface, and underwater battle spaces. Certain capabilities such as satellite intelligence and communications, electromagnetic spectrum superiority, air support and air operations, surface warfare and anti-submarine warfare, require long-time trainings and cannot be integrated in a short time. As a result, it is still unlikely for Chinese Navy to develop enough strength capable of competing with the US Navy within the Second Island Chain in next decade.

Secondly, regarding the potential military conflict over the Diaoyutai/Senkaku Islands, one has to understand why Chinese government reacted so strongly to the issue in recent years. When China and Japan signed the Sino-Japanese Peace and Friendship Treaty in 1972, both sides agreed to set aside the Diaoyutai/Senkaku dispute and leave it for future leaders to find a proper solution. Thus Chinese bottom-line is to keep the issue "undecided." As long as Japanese government does not challenge Chinese position, Beijing will not react strongly to the Diaoyutai/Senkaku dispute. Yet Japanese government's decision to nationalizing Diaoyutai Islands in 2012 was interpreted by Beijing as move to change the *status quo* of the dispute.

On a potential conflict over Diaoyutai/Senkaku Islands, China has more choices for operation. In additional to PLA Navy, Second Artillery and PLA Air Force can also be utilized for combat situations. Given China's military superiority within First Island Chain, when a limited conflict with Japan breaks out, Japanese forces deployed around Diaoyutai /Senkaku may not be able to effectively stand against Chinese missile attacks because China is capable of suppressing Japan's air-power. It remains unclear if China has an action plan for taking control of Diaoyutai/Senkaku Islands when military clash occurs. If a military clash occurs, both sides are likely to turn down military response and seek a political/diplomatic solution. But if the conflict intensifies and spread to waters near Japanese soil, it will trigger activation of US-Japan military alliance, and US reactions will be expected. Whether and how, the US will intervene will depend on the degree of Japanese actions taken towards the Diaoyutai Island.

Thirdly, when China signed the "Declaration of Conduct of Parties in the South China Sea" with ASEAN countries in 2002, all parties pledged to be self-restraint in South China Sea region and sought for building mutual trust before a final solution be reached. Yet the peaceful atmosphere soon disappeared in 2012 when Philippine naval vessels attempted to arrest Chinese fishermen near the Scarborough Shoal, causing a standoff between Philippine navy and Chinese surveillance ships. Starting in late 2013, China initiated a series of land reclamation projects in Cuarteron Reef, Mischief Reef, Subi Reef, Johnson South

Reef, Fiery Cross Reef, Hughes Reef and Gaven Reefs in the Spratly Islands, an act to demonstrate its determination to deal effectively with the problem of sovereignty over the South China Sea.

The projects of erecting artificial structures on 7 reefs show that China is attempting to build large military bases in the South China Sea. Such developments are unfavorable to other claimants, but it is unstoppable, too. The US and Japan will look closely to the developments and insist the right of free navigation in the areas by sending naval ships to cruise in South China Sea routinely. It is still too early to conclude that China will turn into maritime hegemon in the region because all fortification projects are conducted on reefs occupied by China. It does not violate China's self-claimed policy of not building overseas military projects.

China's intention and interest on the Indian Ocean

All discussions about China's strategic expansion to the Indian Ocean originate from the 2004 report of "Energy Futures in Asia" by US consulting firm Booz Allen Hamilton and prepared for US Defence Department. The report said 'China is adopting a "string of pearls" strategy of bases and diplomatic ties stretching from the Middle East to southern China that includes a new naval base under construction at the Pakistani port of Gwadar.' It further revealed that China's investment in overseas harbors such as Sihanoukville in Cambodia, Sittwe and Coco Islands in Myanmar, Chittagong in Bangladesh, Hambantota in Sri Lanka, and Gwadar in Pakistan, symbolized China's interest in the Indian Ocean. Using facilities and infrastructures in these harbors, Chinese naval task groups could operate in the Indian Ocean for long periods, and can therefore ensure the transit safety of energy and commerce. One can understand China's strategic objectives in the Indian Ocean by analyzing following two questions:

1. Is it possible for a single country like China to acquire enough capability of securing the entire Sea Lane of Communication (SLOC)?

2. What are China's strategic interests in sending fleet into the Indian Ocean?

First of all, the energy security is vital to China because it will affect China's economic growth. Currently China import crude oil primarily from the Middle East and Africa with 80 percent of the oil import passing through the Strait of Malacca. Geographically, India is the most important country along China's oil route in the Indian Ocean, but even superpower like US is not able to control global maritime transportation alone, not to mention India. Currently Chinese navy remains unable to conduct sea control operations in the Indian Ocean and secure the SLOCs alone and will never acquire such capability. To carry out long-range escort missions, it is necessary to have logistic support from overseas forward operating bases with suitable piers (depth and berth), emergency repair facilities, logistic support for oil and ammunition, and protection against air, surface and underwater threats, command and control, intelligence and surveillance capabilities.

Comparing to Indian navy and air force, China's aircraft carrier task group does not have enough air power to defend itself in the high seas. The only option for China is to make alliance with Pakistan against India, forcing the latter to give up the tradition of being the dominant power in the Indian Ocean. This option looks unlikely due to political instabilities in Pakistan in recent years. Instead of building long-range naval capability, China seems more interested in building political and diplomatic cooperation with countries along Indian Ocean to protect its maritime interests. That explains why China never recognized the existence of "String of Pearls" strategy, but proposed to build Maritime Silk Road after Xi Jinping came to power.

From this perspective, one can conclude that China's intention to sending naval fleets to cruise in the Gulf of Aden on regular basis is to conduct trainings and gain experiences for its naval fleet, rather than an attempt to projecting its combat capabilities into Indian Ocean. India and China will probably compete in terms of overall naval capabilities, but a confrontation in India Ocean looks unlikely in near future.

Analysis and concluding remarks

In 2006, China, Vietnam and Laos completed the trilateral border junction point treaty, which means China had completed settling 90 percent of the boundary lines with neighbouring countries (especially the eastern boundary line of demarcation between China and Russia), leaving India and Bhutan the remaining two neighbours with undecided borders with China. At same time, Russian government under the leadership of President Vladimir Putin actively developed a closer partnership with China. These developments signify that traditional land-based threat originated from north is now alleviated. Since then China began to redirect its military development toward the sea.

Since 2000, Chinese Navy started building new warships capable of conducting long-range operations. The purpose is to expand its navel influence beyond territorial waters. In 2007, Chinese navy began to conduct military exercises within First and even Second-Island Chains, which were interpreted by US as a serious challenge to the regional stability. However, China has repeatedly claimed in all their Defence white papers that it would never seek hegemony and never adapt expansionism.

In 2012, Chinese government declared territorial-water baseline on the Diaoyutai/Senkaku Islands, an act signifies China's assertion to defending its maritime interests. China's actions seemed more assertive when comparing with the attitude towards land-based disputes, particularly with India, but this development also led to more confrontation with Japan, which soon decided to strengthen military ties with the US. Japan and US are probably the closest allies since the signing of security treaty in 1960. In South China Sea, China's stand-offs with other claimants and fortification projects on its reefs also suffer similar consequences. Claimants like the Philippines and Vietnam moved closer to the US, trying to get US forces back to the region to counterbalance rising Chinese influence. By asserting the right of free navigation and sending naval vessels to cruise in the region, US successfully challenged Chinese position of claiming entire South China Sea to be Chinese territories.

China's assertive actions in Diaoytai/Senkaku and South China Sea will inevitably lead to a direct confrontation with the US. When Chinese President Xi Jinping made his first visit to US in June 2013, he formally expressed that the Pacific Ocean is big enough to accommodate two great powers, meaning China had no intention to confront with US in the Pacific. But the US reactions to China's assertive actions on East and South China Seas imply that Washington D.C. remains reluctant to accept Chinese proposal for power sharing on the West Pacific.

China's strategy in the Indian Ocean is somewhat different. Given the fact that no single country is able to control SLOCs, it will be impossible for China to assume hegemon on Indian Ocean. Besides, Chinese naval fleet or aircraft carrier task group does not even have enough capability to conduct combat independently on high seas. That explains why China started sending naval fleets to Indian Ocean since 2008—the purpose is to acquire experiences for conducting missions on high seas. Instead of building projective capability on Indian Ocean, China seems more interested in building political and diplomatic cooperation with countries along Indian Ocean to protect its maritime interests. That is why Chinese President Xi Jinping formally proposed Maritime Silk project in recent years. It will take time for one to assess if the strategy will succeed.

Understanding China's MSR Initiative: A Perspective in the context of IOR-Pacific Security and Economic Cooperation

Prof Yang Minghong

Introduction

This paper provides an analysis of the Chinese Government's "Twenty-first Century Maritime Silk Road Initiative" within the wider context of Chinese discourses on security and economic cooperation in the Indo-Pacific Region. In 2013, the Chinese Government announced its plan to initiate a vast and far-reaching array of initiatives aimed at fostering increased economic connectivity between the Asia-Pacific Region, the countries around the Indian Ocean, and Europe. Under the umbrella terms like "Twenty-first Century Maritime Silk Road", initiative embody China's strategic conception to build and shape multiple trade routes between the regions, increase competition, and create more opportunities for economic cooperation with countries along the route. Since the inception of the Initiative, however, concerns have risen about its impact on regional security. Some countries anticipate an increased potential for international conflict in the Indo-Pacific Region as a direct result of China's economic and political influence being fostered through this initiative. This paper will examine these discourses and position the Initiative within a context of the wider framework of regional security. The paper will then focus on an analysis of the motivations that have - from a Chinese perspective - informed the Initiative, namely: the vision of a sustainable cooperation between China and other countries, and the building of mechanisms for regional cooperation on economy and security.

In 2013, the Chinese Government announced its plan to initiate a vast and far-reaching array of initiatives aimed at fostering economic connectivity between the Asia-Pacific Region, the countries around the Indian Ocean, and Europe. Under the term "Twenty-first Century Maritime Silk Road", these initiatives embody China's strategy to build and shape multiple trade routes between the regions, increase competition, and create more opportunities for economic cooperation with countries along the route. Since the inception of the Initiative, however, concerns have risen about its impact on regional security. Some countries anticipate an increased potential for international conflict in the Indo-Pacific Region as a direct result of China's economic and political influence being fostered through this initiative. There have been some doubts related to MSR in India: Is the intention of China's "MSR"initiative not clear? Is the Initiative not transparent? Will it squeeze India's strategic space? Here I will examine these discourses and position the initiative within a context of the wider framework of regional security.

Is the Strategic Intention of China's «MSR» Initiative not clear?

Many people in India believe that the strategic intention of Chinese government's initiative to build "MSR" is not clear. Because of its ambiguity, many people are over-interpreting it. I would like to talk a little bit about its history.

In the late 1990s, there is a discourse in USA, in which China was trying to use trade port facilities around the world to control the"strategic tunnels". In early 2005, an internal report of US Department of Defence, titled"Energy Future of the Asia", said that China was taking a "string of pearls"strategy, "China is trying to establish strategic relations with the countries along the sea lanes from Middle East to South China Sea, indicating its offensive and Defence posture which is aimed at protecting the energy interests of China and serving its wide range of safety goals ". A report from India on February 4, 2013, said that Pakistan's Gwadar port will become an important part of China's "string of pearls strategy", China's strategic position in the Persian Gulf and the Arabian Sea will be improved. On February 13, 2014,a website "The diplomat"in Japan linked China's"MSR"intiative with Western's speculation of China's "string of pearls strategy", regarding it as China's strategy for the Indian Ocean expansion. In this context, "MSR" initiative was interpreted as China's "string of pearls strategy", namely "strategic Encirclement" aiming at India.

I think the intention of "MSR" Initiative is clear. On March 28, 2015, State Councilor Yang Jiechi at the annual meeting of the Boao Forum for Asia pointed out that "building the 21st Century Maritime Silk Road is the continuation and development of the ancient maritime Silk Road", and he clearly defined it from "continuation" and "development" as the two aspects. According to his speech, "What we want to continue is the Silk Road spirit featuring peace, friendship, openness, inclusiveness, mutual learning and mutual benefit", "What we want to develop is to properly design cooperation pivots and economic corridors on the sea for all-round maritime cooperation in this age of economic globalization and multipolarity. While upholding its own maritime rights and interests, China stands ready to work together with other countries to build maritime partnerships of win-win cooperation" .Meanwhile, Yang Jiechi further clarified and reiterated that "it is by no means a tool for any country to seek geopolitical advantages. Rather, it is a public goods for all countries. It will tolerate no monopoly or coercion of whatever form. Rather, everyone is equally treated while business is conducted through consultation. "

The authoritative official document *Vision and Actions on Jointly Building Silk Road Economic Belt and 21st-Century Maritime Silk Road* explicitly pointed out that the purpose of "one Belt and one Road Initiative" is to instill vigor and vitality into the ancient Silk Road, to connect Asian, European and African countries more closely and promote mutually beneficial cooperation to a new hight and in new forms. It predicted that "accelerating the building of one Belt and one Road can help promote the economic prosperity of the countries along the Belt and Road and regional economic cooperation, strengthen exchanges and mutual learning between different civilizations, and promote world peace and development. It is a great undertaking that will benefit people around the world."In one word,the intention of China's initiative to build MSR» is clear.

Is the strategic policy of China's MSR imitative not transparent?

Some scholars in India believe that the strategic policy of "the 21st century Maritime Silk Road Initiative" is not clear, and couldn't find the entrance to participate. But from the Chinese government's official document the *"Vision and Actions on Jointly Building Silk Road Economic Belt and 21st-Century Maritime Silk Road"* and the Chinese leadership's remarks, its strategic policy is transparent. Here are some areas which need further analysis:

Firstly, the cooperation mainly covers the economic, cultural and humanlities exchanges. On March 28, 2015, State Councilor Yang Jiechi at the annual meeting of the Boao Forum for Asia pointed out that "In addition to maritime transport and resource development, it will involve research, environmental protection, tourism, disaster reduction and prevention, law enforcement cooperation and people-to-people exchanges on the sea. Not only will it look at the development of the blue economy and building of oceanic economic demonstration zones offshore, it will also build onshore industrial parks, marine science and technology parks and training bases for ocean-related personnel. Not only will we go utilizing the oceanic resources, we will also protect well our oceanic environment."Thus, the framework of "MSR" is mainly economic and trade cooperation and cultural exchanges, military cooperation are excluded from the initiative.

Secondly, the cooperation stressed connectivity. Connectivity is not about one party accepting the plan made by another, or one party following the rules set by another. It is instead an exercise of looking for common ground and areas of cooperation on the basis of mutual respect, leading to the formulation of a joint plan. At the same time, connecting the development strategy to the countries along the belt may help many of India's development strategies as it can be connected to the "MSR". Modi's across the Indian Ocean Maritime Routes and Cultural Landscape Plan have similarities to China's MSR Initiative, These plan from India,I believe,is aiming at reviving the ancient Indian maritime routes and cultural ties with the Indian Ocean countries. I donot think India's idea is exclusive. Moreover, it is connecting the project with enterprises. Quite a few Asian and European countries are stepping up port and infrastructure development, expanding shipping, fishing and fish processing industries and planning industrial parks, special zones, bonded areas and free trade zones near their ports. There are many such projects in the pipeline and with good market prospects. Chinese companies have both experience and capability in these fields. We suggest that governments could facilitate business partnerships by helping our enterprises to match up their projects so that they can complement each other while sharing risks and gains.

Thirdly, The purpose of the "MSR" is to realize infrastructure interconnection, therefore infrastructure constructions become very important. The establishment of Asian Infrastructure Investment Bank, BRICS Development Bank and Silk Road Fund provide a strong material base for the countries along the line. The port construction is mainly for civilian use and is used to develop economy and trade. Chinese domestic scholars estimated that these ports are within India's missile strike, and did not pose any threat to India. Normal supply of Chinese warships can be fed in any port as long as it in accordance with international law. Indian warships to visit South China Sea can be fed at any port, provided that it accord with the international law.

Ports	Countries
Chittagong	Bangladesh
Sittwe port	Burma
Hambantota port, Colombo port	Sri Lanka
Gwadar port	Pakistan
Bagamoyo port	Tanzania
Kuantan Port	Malaysia

Table 1: Ports that China intent to cooperate and construct in the Indian Ocean
Source:website

Fourthly, the key is the mechanism construction. There are many bilateral and multilateral mechanisms and platforms in the Western

Pacific-Indian Ocean, such as Shanghai Cooperation Organization(SCO). These multilateral cooperation mechanisms can play an constructive role to attract more countries and regions participate in the construction of the "MSR". Moreover, many platforms like Boao Forum for Asia, can also play an active role. From above, the strategic policy of the "MSR" is transparent, it is not a conspiracy of economic first and then military follows.

Will China's MSR imitative squeeze India's strategic space?

In 2012, India's well-known strategist C.Raja Mohan made three basic arguments -refer to Sino-Indian relations in his new book "Samudra Manthan, Sino-Indian Rivalry in the Indo-Pacific": First, competition between China and India is sustained; Second, Sino-Indian traditional overland competition will "spill over" into the sea; Third,Indo-Pacific will become a new geographical space. In addition, some Indian scholars doubt that "Will Maritime Silk Road squeeze India's strategic space?" In my opinion, there are four points worth discussing:

Firstly, the maritime trade competitive situation has a long history. Before "MSR"initiative, China and the countries along Indian Ocean has always had friendly exchanges and cooperation in the economic, trade and humanities, both input resources to the region, and also had competition in economic and trade, it is not after Chinese government proposed to build the "MSR" that formed the competitive situation.

Secondly, the competition will mainly occur in economy and trade, instead of other areas. The Maritime Silk Road in history was a maritime trade network which consisted of a series of ports between East Asia and east coast of Africa, Quanzhou in Fijian Province as a starting point in east, through South-East Asia, India and the Arabian Peninsula. These formed a highly prosperous prospect for the late Tang to Song Dynasty, promoted the exchange of trade, spread of geographic knowledge and trade navigation technology. In ancient times, it witnessed the peaceful and friendly exchanges between China, South Asia and South-East Asia, also reflected that even at that powerful time, China had good-friendly relations with neighbouring countries, focusing on equality of economic and trade exchanges. It is completely different from colonialism in Europe. In modern times, China pursues active Defence policy, there is no evidence to show that China has or is changing this policy, turning into expansionary policy. China and India, as Asian countries, were deeply affected by the colonialist invasion, China could understand India's vigilant mind, worrying that China's purpose is to open maritime trade routes.

Thirdly, competition under the premise of promoting cooperation has a positive effect in this region. China's MSR initiative stressed the building of mutually beneficial win-win "interests community" and "destiny community". The present of "Interests community" and "destiny community" suggested that China has put China and other countries' economic competition on the premise of cooperation. From this perspective, we would see there are both cooperation and competition in this region, but we should avoid vicious competition, competition on the premise of cooperation can help to improve the economic viability of this region.

Fourthly, China will not monopolize the benefits of "MSR". February 13, 2015, Chinese Foreign Ministry spokesman Hua Chunying pointed out that the reason why China proposed the building of the Maritime Silk Road is to explore the unique values and ideas from the ancient Silk Road, that is "learning from each other" and giving new era connotation to it, realizing joint development and common prosperity of all countries in the region. This is a cooperation initiative and cooperation concept, through the "MSR" we can integrate various ongoing cooperation with the Silk Road concept and spirit, especially interconnection cooperation. Thus interconnected we can accelerat our development. In short MSR will not squeeze India's strategic space.

Conclusion

The strategic concept of the "MSR" came from the history, connecting China and foreign countries, complying with peace, development, cooperation and win-win trend of the times, carrying the dreams of development and prosperity along the Silk Road, giving new era connotation to the ancient Silk Road. From a historical perspective, China has a long tradition of marine civilization, since the Ming Dynasty and Qing Dynasty boycott and other reasons, maritime exchange declined and the South Asian route was gradually dominated by European countries, and colonialism became a passage to Asia, which is one of the reasons that Chinese Modern trend fall behind other countries. What the Chinese want to do is to restore the marine cultural heritage, exploring business and culture resources, taking more emphasis on "peace, cooperation and prosperity", combining China's "self-interest" and "altruism" to develop marine economy.

It is clear that the strategic intention and policy of China's "MSR" Initiative is not ambiguous, and China's MSR initiative will not squeeze India's strategic space. Therefore, attitudes to China's MSR initiative could be put into consideration in the following way: Firstly to abandon "Cold War" mindset, and make friends with other countries. Secondly to abandon a "zero sum game" strategy, but implement a "win-win" strategy. Thirdly, establishing the vision of sustainable cooperation between China and other countries, and setting up economic and security mechanisms for regional cooperation.

PART – II

Dynamics of Cooperation, Competition and Conflict in the Indian Ocean

Dynamics of Competition, Cooperation and Conflict in South East Asia (SEA)

Lt Gen Datuk Azizan Bin Md Delin

Introduction

I have been assigned to speak on the big "C"s which is on the dynamics of Competition, Cooperation and Conflict in South East Asia. I believe this topic is threefold; and as such choose to address what are the probable causes of conflict in the SEA region before moving on to the competition and cooperation dynamics.

Conflict and the Security Scenario in the SEA Region

Southeast Asia remains a region of interest for many countries; due to its strategic location, and its resources. The Straits of Malacca retains a position of critical strategic and economic importance. The South China Sea is another vital sea lane of communication, connecting the Indian and Pacific Ocean, and harbouring potentially large energy reserves. With a history of non-traditional security threats, and tensions over disputed islands, it remains an area of concern for Malaysia and our international partners. So too, is the various non-state conflicts in our region – from the Southern Philippines to Southern Thailand. I believe that the growing global interest in Asia and Southeast Asia brings opportunities as well as risks.

Security issues in the region are also becoming very delicate and if not addressed carefully may turn into a potential flashpoint in the competition for supremacy amongst the superpowers. This is in reference to the situation in the maritime domain of the South China Sea with China's rise and the US freedom of navigation belief. Also, South-East Asia's strategic location as a crossroad of the world's commerce, ideas and civilisations means that conflicts from elsewhere can easily spread to our shores. Other recent issues like the Rohingya refugee crisis remain a security and humanitarian concern for countries in ASEAN.

Meanwhile, both natural and man-made disasters continue to affect the SEA region more frequently than ever before. The recent haze which affected Indonesia, Malaysia and Singapore significantly, as well as parts of Thailand, Brunei and Southern Philippines clearly indicates that trans-border environmental issues require all of us to work even more closely than ever before. Natural disasters will also occur in areas and at times when one least expect them to happen, such as what Malaysia experienced in the Sabah earthquake in June this year. This incident impacted 187 climbers of various nationalities and took the lives of 18 climbers of five nationalities including those from Malaysia and Singapore. Other calamities such as the recent floods in Myanmar, the frequent typhoons in the Philippines as well as earthquakes in the region certainly require a more concerted effort from all of us in assisting those in their hour of need.

The Evolving Security Threat

The world is a very different place now and likewise, threats to security has changed dramatically especially in light of earth-shaking events like the 9/11 attacks, the Arab Spring and now the rise of the IS. The biggest threat to nation states today I believe is not so much from each other but from non-state actors and as is often the case they are transnational entities. These come in many forms, from religious extremists to cyber terrorists. The spread of information and communication technology has united the world and reaching out to each other is easier than ever before. But it has also provided terrorists and criminals a new way to communicate, plan attacks and launder money. Worse still, new communication platforms especially through social media networks such as Facebook, YouTube, Twitter, and even Whats App have allowed these terrorists plenty of avenues to spread their twisted message of hatred.

We are, ironically, despite the increased affordability of mobile data the world over, paying a heavy price by living in a hyper-connected world.

Of a more prominent threat to all of us now are the IS and its followers. Indeed the overall threat of terrorism is greatly amplified by today's hyper-connected and interlinked world, where an incident in one corner of the globe can instantly spark a reaction thousands of miles away. What we have feared all this while has come to reality - the threat of terrorists that is increasingly decentralized, difficult to track and so becoming difficult to prevent. Incidents in Sydney and Paris early this year, Bangkok's Erawan Shrine in August and the heinous recurrence in Paris last Friday (13th Nov 15) clearly indicate that it is almost impossible to predict and pre-empt a terrorist attack despite numerous security measures in place.

I wish to highlight another disturbing trend which is the explicit use of the cyber domain by terrorists. Even more alarming are the widespread visual releases by these groups depicting bombings, mass executions and beheadings in multiple languages. The fight against terrorism will be a long and difficult one and, defeating it will take a long time, not simply with military might alone. It will require the multilateral participation of many governments, militaries and agencies to eliminate or reduce the possibility of terrorist operations, especially from establishing operating bases across the borders and within our territories.

Cooperating for peace in the region

As one of the five founding members, Malaysia's foreign policy cannot be understood without ASEAN. We believe that a strong and successful ASEAN is not only an economic necessity, but also a strategic imperative. The institutions that ASEAN leads, such as the ASEAN Plus One Dialogue Process, the ASEAN Regional Forum, the ASEAN Defence Ministers Meeting Plus and the East Asia Summit are critical. They provide the necessary platform to promote confidence, transparency and the developments of rules and norms. Even as I speak, the 27th ASEAN Summit and related summit meetings are being held in Kuala Lumpur from 18th to 22nd Nov 15.

Through ASEAN, member states have substantially reduced intra-regional threats. ASEAN provides a forum for conflict resolution and a bridge to security problems in the wider world, besides strengthening the bonds between members. As Malaysia knows from experience, those bonds are needed most and tested most in difficult times. In February 2013, there was an armed intrusion in LahadDatu, driven by a misguided belief to lay claim on the state of Sabah in East Malaysia. After initially seeking a peaceful resolution to the violence, we were forced to react with military force. These men were attempting to enforce what they believed was a centuries-old claim to the state. In the subsequent operations, 'Daulat' to repel the intruders, 71 Sulu Intruders were killed at the expense of 10 Malaysian Security personnel who were killed in action. In the aftermath, we established the Eastern Sabah Security Command, which works to strengthen maritime security in the area.

There are many lessons that could be gained from this incident. Certainly one that is most prominent is the threat from non-state actors, in a non-traditional manner. The incident shows that the biggest threats to nations today are not always from each other, but from shadowy groups, often with historical grievances not easily addressed. These groups recognize no national boundaries, are often not easily categorized and whose motivations are often unclear or shifting. The LahadDatu incident also reinforced the need for close cooperation with our neighbours, particularly the Philippines in assisting us during the height of the crisis. I am pleased to note that we were able to repay the favour and demonstrate our own commitment to lasting peace in the region in the negotiations for the Comprehensive Agreement on Bangsamoroin 2014. Malaysia is honoured to have facilitated the final deal between the Government of the Philippines and the Moro Islamic Liberation Front; the culmination of many years of hard work, and an enduring commitment to peace. The Agreement is a clear example of how close cooperation and camaraderie can overcome conflicts, and dampen potential flashpoints in the region. Cooperation with nations beyond ASEAN – including those who have the capabilities to address multi-dimensional security threats – remains a critical part of our regional security.

At the regional and international level, we must explore ways to make a bigger contribution to the world's primary security challenges: non-proliferation, conflict resolution and peace-building, terrorism and piracy. As an example, the Malacca Straits patrol (which comprises of the *Malacca Strait Sea Patrol*, the "*Eyes in the Sky*" air patrols and the *Intelligence Exchange Group* is a set of cooperative security measure undertaken by Malaysia, Indonesia, Singapore and Thailand to ensure the security of merchant ships as they sail from the Andaman Sea into the Straits of Malacca and vice-versa. Related to this, India established the *Far East Naval Command* (FENC) and attains the 'Hawk-eye' in the maritime area north of the Straits of Malacca to secure its mainland from any threats and actively participated with Thailand to ensure Joint – Air patrols. India's close naval engagement with the navies of this region including Malaysia is also a positive outlook for the security in the Straits of Malacca. Other initiatives such as the inaugural **South and South East Asian Nations (SASEAN**) Defence Chiefs' Dialogue held in Sri Lanka last year certainly promote regional peace and stability through dialogues and cooperation. This forum for the Defence Chiefs of Asia is expected to reinforce the vision of The Conference on Interaction and Confidence Building Measures in Asia (CICA).

I also reiterate my belief that addressing the threats posed by terrorists would require multi-faceted and integrated measures which must also include addressing the roots of these evil. In Malaysia for example, there are already measures in place in the *"de-radicalisation"* of extremists and militants undertaken by the police and religious authorities. This experience was shared early last month during the *Special ASEAN Ministers Meeting on the Rise of Radicalisation and Violent Extremism* **(SAMMRRVE)** in Kuala Lumpur. Early last month at the Leaders' Summit on Countering ISIL and Violent Extremism at the UN, Malaysia's Prime Minister Dato' Seri Najib Razak initiated the call for ASEAN governments to come up with an organised strategy to counter the lies being spread by IS online, supposedly in the name of Islam. I am also pleased to note that ASEAN and China will soon have MOU to combat cybercrimes which was agreed at the ASEAN Ministerial Meeting on Transnational Crime (AMMTC) recently. Malaysia was also proposed by the US as the regional Digital Counter-Messaging Communications Centre to prevent the spread of IS ideology and propaganda through the internet. With these developments, we can all work together in a concerted effort to dispel and counter the distorted belief posed by the IS. The concept of moderation which Malaysia have championed and accepted as an ASEAN way could also be integrated in the cyber domain. This is where a more balanced and moderate approach can be inculcated not only in our dealings with each other but also as to how we conduct our daily lives.

Conclusion

In conclusion, I believe the risk of conflict between nations and in particular ASEAN member states seem remote and unthinkable now. South-East Asia which has seen war, occupation and terrorism in its past knows all too well the cost of conflict, and why it shouldn't be allowed to fester. Therefore, South-East Asia has a real and crucial stake in the movement to prevent conflict throughout the globe. The harmony and economic prosperity that the people of ASEAN have enjoyed did not come easily. We have laboured hard to achieve what we have today. It is the fruit of the sown seeds of constructive cooperation, respect and mutual trust that has developed over time. Moreover, as the fulcrum of global economic growth, the need for peace and stability in our region is crucial, not only for our countries, but the world as a whole. By working with our friends and neighbours, we can choose to share the dividends of stability and not the cost of conflict.

Middle East Competition Dynamics Little Cooperation Much Conflict

Commodore Lalit Kapur (Retd)

Introduction

What comes to mind when one thinks of the Middle East? Among the images that the term generates (in no particular order) are the partition of the Ottoman Empire and the secretive Sykes-Picot plan that led to artificial kingdoms being created and propped up in pursuit of Anglo-French interests; the cynical use of war by Western oil industry to serve its commercial purposes; USA trying to manage Arab – Israeli conflict to keep the region stable; peace gripped by a morass of oil and unable to take wing; Iran's search for nuclear weapons and apprehensions that the recent US-Iran N-deal will eventually help in this search; extremist organisations like the ISIS that were created and supported for geopolitical ends but are now out of control and wreaking havoc within the civilian population of the region; AylanKurdi and the refugee crisis that has gripped Europe, while destroying the lives of the people of Syria and Iraq; and the unwillingness of oil-rich Arab states to provide refuge to the people finding their way to a more peaceful world – after all, why should they, after seeing what happened in Lebanon? The Middle East has become synonymous with instability, misrule and cynical geopolitics, with little to show by way of cooperation and much conflict of every type.

The term "Middle East" was first used by Rear Adm Alfred Thayer Mahan, in his essay "The Persian Gulf and International Relations", published in the September 1902 issue of London's 'Monthly Review'[1]. The term as used by Mahan referred to Persia, now Iran. It has expanded to include the Western part of Asia without the Caucasus, but including Egypt, the non-Maghreb part of Africa. Geographically, the area links Europe, the erstwhile Soviet Union (now Russia and the Central Asian Republics), the Indian sub-continent and Africa. It has only three outlets into the world's oceans, in the Mediterranean, Red Sea and the Persian Gulf. Except Iran, Turkey and Egypt, the numerous states comprising the Middle East are artificial constructs, created in the last century or so.

Economically, it is the world's richest source of exportable energy and thus vital for growing energy dependent economies: as per the BP Statistical Review of World Energy June 2015, West Asia's proven oil reserves at the end of 2014 stood at 109.7 billion tones or 810.7 billion barrels, 47.7 percent of the world's proven reserves[2]. Production in 2014 was over 28.5 million barrels per day, 31.7 percent of global production[3]. Reserves of natural gas stood at 79.8 trillion cubic metres, 42.7 percent of global reserves[4]. Of the total global oil trade of 56.7 million barrels per day (mbpd) in 2014, 22.9 mbpd, more than 40 percent of the world total, went to Asia. Geographically, it remains the link between Europe as well as the East Coast of the Americas and Asia, with the Suez Canal being used by the overwhelming majority of all shipping (and therefore trade). In the religious domain, the region is predominantly Islamic, with nearly 300 million out of the world Muslim population of 1.6 billion living in West Asia. The rise of Islamic extremism automatically makes this region a focal area. Demographically, it has only about 4 percent of the world's population, increasing at roughly 1.4 percent every year. Turkey and Iran are the biggest population centers, each has about 75 million. Iraq and Saudi Arabia are the next biggest, with a population of about 32 million each. Explosive economic growth in the latter half of the 20th century resulted in the region attracting large numbers of expatriates who remit huge quantities of foreign exchange to their parent nations and will inevitably remain a concern for them. Ethnically, it is home to the Arab, Persian, Turkic and Jewish communities, with Kurds being the major ethnic group without their own state, resulting in their being spread in Iran, Iraq, Syria and Turkey.

George Santayana, philosopher, novelist, essayist and poet had said, "Those who cannot remember the past are condemned to repeat it"[5]. Human beings live their lives looking forward, constantly being surprised by developments and not understanding the underlying reasons. A study of history, otherwise described as a carefully constructed collective memory, is vital to understanding of geo-political developments. The Middle East is currently experiencing multiple conflicts, whose root causes can be traced, among others, to the following:-

- Self-serving actions of the colonial powers.

- Unraveling of the post-Ottoman state system, which in turn has led to a struggle for control of Islam with its Sunni-Sunni and Sunni-Shia conflicts, the Arab Spring and independence movements.

- Continuing competition for control of oil and gas.

- The Arab Israeli divide.

Actions of Colonial Powers

When asked how Britain could help resolve the conflict over Kashmir during his visit to Pakistan in April 2011, PM David Cameron is reported to have said, "I don't want to insert Britain in some leading role where, as with so many of the world's problems, we are responsible for the issue in the first place"[6]. This thought applies equally to the Middle East. While it would be incorrect to hold Britain directly responsible for much of the conflict plaguing the Middle East, their interference and self-serving policies are acknowledged by many historians as being among the root causes of conflict in the region. Two examples will be cited in this paper: one of Egypt and the Suez Canal, the other dealing with competition for oil.

Egypt

The opening of the Suez Canal in 1869 made Egypt vital ground for Britain and France, cutting down transit time to their Indian Ocean possessions substantially. Despite initially having opposed construction of the canal, Britain bought Egypt's 44% shareholding in 1875, becoming the canal company's largest shareholder. Khedive Ismail Pasha, the de facto ruler of Egypt (although technically an autonomous province of the Ottoman Empire, Egypt was for all practical purposes independent) ran up huge debts amounting to over £100 million, which resulted in the Anglo-French combine taking control of Egypt's treasury, customs, railways, ports and post offices. A nationalist movement was predictable, and one arose leading eventually to bombardment of Alexandria in 1882 followed by a land invasion to secure control over the Canal. Egypt became a veiled British protectorate and remained one till 1914, when it officially became a British protectorate. The country attained independence only in 1936. Even after independence, Britain retained the right to station troops in Egypt to secure the Canal, the link with their Empire in India. Nationalisation of the Canal in 1956 sparked the Suez Crisis, where Israel, France and Britain jointly invaded Egypt to regain control over the Canal. Strong American, Russian and United Nations opposition forced the invading forces to withdraw, humiliating France and Britain, forcing British Premier Anthony Eden to resign and bringing to an end Great Britain's role as one of the world's great powers.

Competition for Oil

Oil was first discovered at Masjid-i-Suleiman in Iran on 26 May 1908. It sparked an intense competition for control of this resource considered vital for seaborne and military transportation, to an extent that control of oil supplies became a first class British War Aim during WWI. The British forced change of the Sykes-Picot Plan to carve up the Ottoman Empire to ensure they retained Mosul, while USA and France nearly came to conflict with Britain to ensure they received a due share in the oil wealth. After the war, the promises of Arab independence made by the famed Lawrence of Arabia to obtain Arab support against Turkey were dishonoured. Instead, artificial kingdoms with imported rulers were created, giving rise to the states of Iraq, Syria and Jordan, essentially to ensure that control of oil remained with the Western powers. In 1953, the CIA and MI6 came together to depose Iranian Prime Minister Mohammed Mossadegh, essentially because he wanted an audit of the accounts of oil companies. Mohammed Reza Shah Pahlavi was designated to rule "more firmly", leading eventually to the Islamic Revolution in Iran in 1979. USA supported Iraq's Saddam Hussein in his War with Iran, and later, when Saddam was contemplating an invasion of Kuwait, American Ambassador April Glaspie is on record as having told him, "We have no opinion on your Arab-Arab conflicts, such as your dispute with Kuwait[7]". If the first American intervention in Iraq was to depose Saddam, the second was to take control of oil in the region. Even today, USA continues to do in the Middle East much the same that Britain did in the last century – keep the region divided to retain control over the oil.

The reality is that to generate profit, mineral resources have to be both extracted and transported. Extraction requires a politically stable mining site; it the region is unstable, it must be pacified. The British strategy of 'Divide and Rule' ensured no power ever arose that could challenge their supremacy. This policy continues to this day, as a result of which the Arab world is a world divided. Transportation, on the other hand, is cheapest by sea, and if regional nations cannot provide secure transport corridors, extra-regional powers are more than willing to step in to do the needful. An example is the anti-piracy patrols off Somalia. Alan Greenspan, the Chairman of the American Federal Reserve for nearly two decades, is on record as having said, "I am saddened that it is politically inconvenient to acknowledge what everyone knows: the Iraq war was largely about oil"[8]." It is noteworthy that amongst the five vital American interests identified in a study is to "ensure the viability and stability of major global systems (trade, financial markets, supplies of energy and the environment)", and one of the eleven extremely important American interests is "Preventing the emergence of a regional hegemon in important regions, especially the Persian Gulf"[9].

Let us look deeper into transportation of energy. On 31 August 2010, President Obama announced, "the American combat mission in Iraq has ended. Operation Iraqi Freedom is over and the Iraqi people now have lead responsibility for security of their country"[10]. The way was now open for pipelines from the energy rich Gulf to energy hungry Europe. USA backed a pipeline from Qatar through Saudi Arabia,

Jordan and Syria into Turkey. Syria's President Bashar al-Assad, however, supported a pipeline from Iran and Iraq into Syria and thence to Europe through the Mediterranean. This option also suited Russia better. So has sectarian strife and the war in Syria been engineered to provide cover to a war for access to oil and gas, and the wealth that comes with it? If Wikileaks is believed, it has: Julian Assange cites leaked cables from the US State Department to show that USA planned to destabilise Syria and overthrow the Syrian Government as early as 2006[11]. If Syria today faces the nightmare combination of civil war, foreign invasion and terrorism, this has been fomented by Western powers, according to some reports[12]. Syria today is the battleground for multiple conflicts, involving the Syrian Government, rebels, the ISIS, the Al Qaeda affiliate Jabhat al-Nusra, Kurds, USA and its allies, Iraq, Iran and the Hezbollah, Russia, Saudi Arabia and Turkey. Peace is not in sight.

Big power competition in the Middle East continues unabated. The interests of America and its allies have already been highlighted. Russia retains a strategic interest in Tartus, its only naval base in the Mediterranean. It is also extremely concerned about the emergence of an extremist Caliphate in its soft underbelly. China is building a base in the Gulf of Tadjoura, in Djibouti. The competition has turned the Middle East into a cauldron, with numerous states and non-state actors including Al Qaeda, Egypt, Hamas, Hezbollah, Iraq, Iran, the ISIS, Israel, the Palestinian Authority, Saudi Arabia, Syria, Turkey and USA engaged in a complex interplay of conflict and cooperation.

A few words about the ISIS

Who could have imagined that a movement founded by a man who once worked in a video store in provincial Jordan would tear off a third of the territory of Iraq and Syria, shatter all historical institutions and, defeating the combined armies of a dozen of the wealthiest countries on earth, create a mini-empire? Convinced that USA would invade Iraq, Zarqawi began building a base there in 2002, allying with remnants of Saddam's intelligence network. He hit three well-chosen targets by bomb attacks four months after US invasion: the UN HQ in Baghdad, the Jordanian Embassy there and the Imam Ali mosque (Shiite) in

Najaf, ensuring there would be no Shia-Sunni reconciliation. His plan to cleave Iraq was ready in 2003, when USA was still denying that there was in insurgency in Iraq. Pleas from tribal elders, as in Fallujah, for protection against Zarqawi were ignored by USA. Some Americans even said that the answer for Iraq was an 80 percent solution, ignoring the 20 percent Sunni population and creating a new state involving the remaining 80 percent Shias and Kurds.Zarqawi himself was killed in American airstrike in June 2006, but his followers declared the Islamic state of Iraq in October 2006 and launched sectarian war against Iraqi Shias, while USA remained in denial. The American troop surge all but killed movement founded by Zarqawi, but embers remained and were nurtured at US prison camps where Sunni devotees mingled with former members of Saddam's Baath party, creating a new movement. Iraq actually voted the corrupt Maliki out of power in 2010, but USA contrived a horse-trading agreement that kept Maliki in power. After Maliki's "re-election", IS went on assassination spree, removing all Sunni opposition to their policies. Neither Maliki nor USA cared. This assassination campaign weakened Sunni opposition and helped ISIS seize Mosul in 2014. ISIS was then strengthened by seven major prison raids, including on Abu Ghraib that added several thousand fighters to its ranks. As admitted by Lt Gen James Clapper, Director of National Intelligence, "We underestimated ISIL and overestimated fighting capacity of the Iraqi Army. I didn't see the collapse of the Iraqi Security Force in the North coming"[13]. The capture of Mosul led to USA forcing replacement of Maliki with a less sectarian PM. But America had lost trust of Sunni elders who could create a force to roll back the ISIS. The US backed legislation that would create a Sunni National Guard in Iraq remains stalled in Iraq's Shia dominated parliament. An air campaign may send ISIS leaders underground, but they will inevitably emerge again unless a mechanism that looks after Sunni interests in Iraq is created.

Other conflicts include the abortive Arab Spring which at one stage provided glimpses of the possibility of representative governments emerging in the Middle East, the Arab-Israeli Conflict, and the Sunni-Shia conflict for leadership of the Islamic world. The future appears bleak. The West has been taken by surprise twice, first by the emergence of Al Qaeda in 1998 and now by emergence of the ISIS. The crisis has the potential of going out of control, plunging the entire region into ferment. There are no signs of a united region emerging, and in any case, such a united region would be against Western interests. China and India have already emerged as the largest customers of oil and gas for the Middle East; in fact the irony is that the biggest customers of Middle East energy are dependent upon those whose short-sighted policies created the problem in the first place to solve it. Will Asia Pacific powers take on a greater role in conflict management in the region?

Conclusion

It must be acknowledged that transportation and security for the Middle East have historically been provided by the West. The Middle East regimes remain focused on internal security and this is not likely to change in the foreseeable future. An Indo-Pacific security construct is, therefore, likely to remain a peripheral interest for the Middle East in the years to come.

Endnotes

1. Sahar el-Nadi, in "Middle East of What", in "The European", 18 March 2012, accessed on 12 Nov 15 from http://www.theeuropean-magazine.com/sahar-el-nadi--2/6181-the-long-history-of-a-label. The essay can be accessed from "Retrospect and Prospect – Studies in International Relations" by Capt AT Mahan, published 1902 by Little, Brown and Company, Boston, available at https://ia902604.us.archive.org/12/items/retrospectprospe00maha/retrospectprospe00maha_bw.pdf

2. BP Statistical Review of World Energy June 2015, accessed from https://www.bp.com/content/dam/bp/pdf/energy-economics/statistical-review-2015/bp-statistical-review-of-world-energy-2015-full-report.pdf on 01 Nov 15.

3. Ibid

4. Ibid

5. George Santayana, in "The life of Reason", sourced from http://dictionary. reference.com/browse/those-who-cannot-remember-the-past-are-condemned-to-repeat-it on 11 Nov 2015.

6. James Kirkup and Christopher Hope, in "David Cameron: Britain Caused Many of the World's Problems", published by 'The Telegraph', 05 April 2011, accessed from http://www.telegraph.co.uk/news/politics/david-cameron/8430899/ David-Cameron-Britain-caused-many-of-the-worlds-problems.html on 13 November 2015.

7. New York Times report, 23 September 1990, sourced from https://msuweb. montclair.edu/~furrg/glaspie.html

8. Alan Greenspan, in The Age of Turbulence: Adventures in a New World

9. America's National Interests, as defined by 'The Commission on American National Interests, July 2000", sourced from http://belfercenter.ksg.harvard. edu/files/amernatinter.pdf

10. Remarks by the President in Address to the Nation on the end of Combat Operations in Iraq, sourced from https://www.whitehouse.gov/the-press-office/2010/08/31/remarks-president-address-nation-end-combat-operations-iraq

11. Assange on "US Empire, Assad Government Overthrow Plans and New Book", sourced from https://www.rt.com/news/314852-assange-wikileaks-us-syria/

12. For example see MnarMuhawesh, "Migrant Crisis and Syria Civil War Fuelled by Competing Gas Pipelines", sourced from http://www.mintpressnews.com/ migrant-crisis-syria-war-fueled-by-competing-gas-pipelines/209294/

13. "US Underestimated Islamic State Militants in Syria – Obama", sourced from https://www.rt.com/usa/191352-obama-underestimated-isis-syria/

PART – III

Dynamics of Cooperation, Competition and Conflict in the Western Pacific

Competition, Conflict and Cooperation and Challenges to management of South China Sea situation

Colonel Nguyen The Hong

Introduction

South China Sea (SCS) is not only one of world's most dynamic economic regions, but is also a source of abundant natural resource, and an important air and maritime route, connecting the Pacific and the Indian Ocean. Therefore, SCS is of increasing geo-political, economic and military importance to neighbouring countries and major countries in the world. SCS is a focal point of conflict in terms of sovereignty and interests among regional countries, which is not only becoming a source of competition among major powers in the world but also has potential risks of collision. Besides securing interests and stability, both foreign and regional countries have strengthened cooperation in order to mitigate the challenges to management of the conflict situations, eliminate potential risks of conflicts, especially military ones in SCS.

Competition, Conflict and Cooperation in SCS

Firstly, due to disagreement over sovereignty and interests, disputes in SCS tend to be more complicated and have potential risks of collision. According to international laws, particularly the United Nations Convention on the Law of the Sea of 1982, based on evidences of history, geography and practical jurisdiction in the SCS, disputes can be classified into two major types:

(1) Disputes amongst China and Vietnam, Malaysia, Philippines, and Brunei, and also between countries who have maritime claims, exclusive economic zone, and continental shelf; (2) Disputes on sovereignty issues over the Paracel and the Spratly Islands, of which the dispute over the Paracel is a bilateral issue between Vietnam and China, while the one in the Spratly is among six parties (China, Vietnam, Philippines, Malaysia, Brunei and Taiwan). Among those parties, China claims its "sovereignty" over the "nine-dash line". On 05 July 2009, China officially expressed views on the international legal implications for the *"nine-dash line"*, which covered 80 percent area of the SCS, which seriously infringed the exclusive economic zones of all other countries, resulting in their opposition. Dispute over sovereignty in SCS is mainly between China and some ASEAN countries, including Vietnam.

Recently, some claimants have strengthened their activities to assert sovereignty and protect their interests in the SCS, causing complexity, potential collision, and conflict in the region:

Firstly, China asserted its sovereignty over the *"nine-dash line"* through activities such as: (1) Establishment of *"Sansha City"*; (2) military training and exercises in SCS, intercepting the US reconnaissance aircraft near Hainan Island, confronting the operations of the US, Philippines aircrafts in the Spratly Islands as well as tracking and impeding activities of US warships in the SCS; (3) seizing foreign fishing ships and all assets onboard, in all areas of China's unilateral claim; (4) surveying and exploring in overlapping waters, and deterring other claimants' surveys and explorations in the areas within the *"ninedash line"*; (5) realizing "initiatives" of regional connectivity. Those activities included: controlling Scarborough Shoal (2012), preventing operations of the Philippines at the Second Thomas Shoal/Spratly Islands, operating Haiyang Shiyou-981 oil rig illegally within Triton/ Paracels area, seriously infringing the exclusive economic zone of Vietnam. In addition, China has speeded up expansion and construction activities on Chinese occupied shoals in Spratly Islands. From late 2013 to now, China has mobilized thousands of workers, a large number of modern facilities to expand and construct infrastructures on seven shoals in Spratly Islands with unprecedented speed and scale, especially at Fierry Cross

Reef, Xubi and Mischief Island. Just over the past year, China has: (1) expanded over 1,000 hectares of occupied shoals in Spratly Islands and continued to do so; (2) China has built 6-8 floor-permanent buildings at Johnson South Reef, Hughes Reef, Cuarter on Reef, and Gaven Reef; (3) constructed a 3,000-meter runway at Fierry Cross Reef, and so on. These activities which China has created risks alteration of the status quo in the SCS; promoting arms race; threatening the peaceful and stable environment in the region; and affecting the marine ecosystem. These have caused concern and strong opposition among the international community. However, despite international and regional reactions, China has been continuing its activities in the Spratly Islands. Chinese Foreign Ministry has held many press conferences and expressed views that *"China's building and expanding the shoals in Spratly Islands are absolutely appropriate, legitimate within its sovereignty, neither prejudicing nor infringing anyone else sovereignty. After completion of the constructions, the functions of Spratly Islands will be more diversified and comprehensive in order to meet indispensable defence needs and serve civilian needs"*.

Recently, due to strategic calculations and reverse impacts of the lawsuit, China has tried to adjust its policy and deployed a series of *"soft"* measures, such as: (1) Through Philippines' diplomatic representative agency, China is trying to convince the Philippines' government to abandon the lawsuit; (2) Implementing "initiatives of connecting region" (applying *"two channels"* approach in resolving SCS issues, *"one belt, one road"* ...), stating its support for the conclusion of the Code of Conduct in the SCS in order to reduce the pressure. However, it still tries to continue accomplishing its strategic objectives, which China had already set in the past.

Secondly, the other claimants in the SCS are trying to strengthen their reactions against China's ambitions. The Philippines and Vietnam strongly reject China's sovereignty violation in the SCS. The Philippines expresses its rigid attitude towards the actions of China, decisively pursues and promotes the litigation. Its lawsuit against China in the International Permanent Arbitration Court is a focus of its SCS policy. The Chinese arbitral tribunal aims to protect China's national sovereignty and to resolve disputes through peaceful means in order not to agitate against or challenge China. Accordingly, right after the Philippine Ministry of Foreign Affairs had submitted the lawsuit against China to the Court, the Philippine Congress issued a resolution supporting the decision of the government, called for its people' solidarity to defend the Philippines' sovereignty in the SCS. The Philippine President declared that it *"would support all necessary things"* in order to carry out the proceedings. In addition, the Philippines: (1) Did not accept "appealing" proposals that China offered; (2) called for the international community to support the case of Philippines, especially countries with maritime disputes with China like ASEAN countries, the US, Japan and the Europe; (3) carried out polls to raise people's consensus and support; (4) hired leading lawyers specializing in maritime law; (5) opposed strongly to China's actions at sea. Malaysia and Indonesia conducted military exercises in the SCS, performed military training in Spratly Islands, and expressed objection to Chinese patrols at Lucconi Shoal, and so on. Indonesia openly declared that there is absolutely no legal basis for the China's *"nine-dash line"*.

Thirdly, the strategic competition between the major powers, makes SCS situations increasingly tense, complex and unpredictable and cause more risks of conflict and challenges peace and stability of the region. In the past, there were only collisions and conflicts among regional countries in the SCS (China with Vietnam, the Philippines, and so on) over sovereignty and interests. However, as the US attaches special importance to the area in its national strategy; the SCS has experienced rapid changes, which are beyond the regions control. It has become a decisive factor in the competition between the US and China in the region. Accordingly, both China and the US have had more aggressive moves in the SCS in order to implement their ambitious strategies, making the SCS situation become tense, complex, unpredictable, and ultimately threatening the regional peace and stability and the interests of other countries in the SCS.

China first and foremost in the Asia-Pacific region is determined to realize its ambition of *"monopolizing the SCS"*, assert its sovereignty over the *"nine-dash line"*, implement the goal of becoming a *"marine power"*, gradually push the US out of the region, and establish itself as a *"world leader"*. Expansion and construction activities in the SCS are the next step in the series of actions that China is pursuing in order to change the status quo in favor of China. Thus China is trying to extend its control, create a legal basis for the *"nine-dash line"* claim, use it as a *"springboard"* to expand military operations and force other countries to follow *"playing rules led"* by China. Meanwhile, the US, who has the ambition of controlling the SCS, has always sought to keep the SCS as a *"hot spot"* to assert its strategic interests. The level of the US's responses to China's activities in the SCS has increased. For example, it raised high-level oppositions as well as other forms of responses; the US ships entered the area within 12 nautical miles from Chinese occupied Shoals in Spratly Islands.

Other major countries are increasingly concerned about their interests in the SCS and have enhanced their competitions with China. Japan has strongly opposed China's activities, as it believes that such activities increase tensions in the SCS. Japan conducted more practical activities to protect its interests, asserted its position in the region, and provided support to some countries who were involved in the disputes with China in the SCS. This was in order to strengthen their capability to defend their sovereignty and maritime security. Russia as well as the EU is also increasingly interested in the SCS. They even have declared that they are ready to participate in joint exercises with some partner countries in the SCS.

In summary, as the SCS has gained geostrategic importance in the national strategies of major countries, especially the US, its allies and China. These countries have promoted activities which increase competition and thus make the situation in the SCS increasingly tense, complex and unpredictable.

However; the countries in the SCS have also tried to strengthened cooperation, through consensus, and tried to peacefully develop this environment. In recent years, the regional countries have conducted many activities to promote cooperation and development, despite nations competing for sovereignty.

As for China, to become a powerful nation in not only this region but in the world, it requires enough space to harness its huge demand for energy for economic development. And for this it requires a peaceful and stable environment. Therefore, on the one hand, it has intrinsic needs for maritime resources; on the other hand, it has needs for cooperation with claimant countries in the SCS. China has been strongly promoting the principle of *"setting aside disputes and pursuing joint development"*. If from this principle, the element of ambitious sovereignty was removed, then this principle has some positive meaning (actually this principle was *"sovereignty belongs to China, setting aside disputes and pursuing joint development"*, but due to other countries' strong reaction, it was changed into *"setting aside disputes and pursuing joint development"*). In recent years, China has issued the *"one axis, two wings"* initiative, including the project of *"expanding Tonkin Gulf economic belt"* and more recently the "initiatives" of connecting the region (the approach of *"two channels"* in resolving SCS issue, *"one belt, one road"*, and so on). Together with the ASEAN, China has declared its support for a Code of Conduct in the SCS in order to implement the policy of *"setting aside disputes and pursuing joint development"* with ASEAN countries and connecting the region.

Other claimant countries have also been actively participating in cooperative and development activities to create consensus, peaceful environment in order to protect their sovereignty and interests in the SCS. Indeed, they have recently conducted many cooperative activities at sea, such as: assigning (fixing, ascertaining) overlapped waters; publishing joint statements and reports; performing cooperative oil and gas exploration and seismic research; cooperating in search and rescue; joint patrols. More specifically:

In the Tonkin Gulf region: Vietnam and China signed the Agreement on Delimitation and Fishing Co-operation in Tonkin Gulf and a framework agreement on cooperation in oil and gas exploration, which was implemented in practice. During the visit to China by Vietnam General Secretary Nguyen PhuTrong from 07 to 10 April 2015, the two countries signed seven agreements, including the agreement on tax issues for the joint exploration project of oil and gas resources in the Gulf of Tonkin between two Ministries of Finance. The two sides also have agreement on joint patrol cooperation. Particularly, the two sides are in talks on the delimitation of the waters outside the mouth of Tonkin Gulf. Negotiations have been held to delimitate waters outside the mouth of Tonkin Gulf.

In Spratly Islands area: Many countries have signed bilateral and multilateral agreements in order to promote and implement the signed agreements, such as three-parties seismic research and oil and gas exploration (Vietnam, the Philippines and China); a joint survey to submit a joint report on limits of the continental shelf beyond 200 nautical miles between Vietnam and Malaysia to the UN Commission on Limits of the Continental Shelf (CLCS) in 2009, and a delimitation agreement between Vietnam and Indonesia on continental shelf (2003). Vietnam and Indonesia have conducted six rounds of talks on the delimitation of the exclusive economic zone within 200 nautical miles at sea between the two countries. From 10 to 12March, 2015 in Indonesia, the 6th round of talks on delimitation of the exclusive economic zone between the two governments was held in accordance to agreement between the leaders of Vietnam and Indonesia. The two sides discussed measures on delimitating exclusive economic zone, and to jointly consider and negotiate in the future.

In addition, apart from the cooperation and agreement on the sovereignty, progress has also been made with great speed, in the fields of economy, science, military and politics. Disputes in the SCS have been becoming a hot topic in many agendas of ASEAN and ASEAN with its partners. ASEAN has issued a lot of joint declarations, statements on the issue of SCS disputes, such as the 1992, 1995 joint declarations, and so on.

Particularly, in 2002, ASEAN and China issued a Declaration on the Conduct of Parties in the SCS to resolve sovereignty dispute through peaceful means, creating a Code of Conduct in order to limit unilateral actions and contribute to regional stability. Defence and military cooperation's in ASEAN, both bilateral and multilateral, have been maintained and developed, thus contributing to the maintenance of peaceful and stable environment in Southeast Asia and the Asia-

Pacific. Cooperation between armed forces of ASEAN countries were conducted in several forms like dialogues between Defence officials, leaders and military commanders about the issues of Defence and security through conferences, talks, forums and visits to each other. The examples are as follows: The ASEAN Chiefs of Army Multilateral Meeting (ACAMM), ASEAN Navy Chiefs Meeting (ANCM), ASEAN Air Forces Chiefs Conference (AACC), ASEAN Chiefs of Defence Forces Informal Meeting (ACDFIM), ASEAN Military Intelligence Informal Meeting (AMIIM); Patrols at sea, such as: joint patrols between Malaysian and Indonesian navies at the Malacca Straits, between Vietnamese and Cambodian navies; between Vietnamese and Thai navies at the Thailand Gulf; bilateral and multilateral exercises among some countries to improve coordination and capability to deal with non-traditional security challenges, such as trans-national crimes, terrorism; joint training; military exchanges; sharing experiences and visits of naval vessels.

Challenges to the Management of the SCS situation

Competition and conflict in the SCS challenges not only the process of promoting cooperation but also the consensus, peaceful development environment and the management of the SCS situation. More specifically:

Firstly, in terms of political and external relations, SCS situation has become tense, complex and unpredictable mainly due to the ambition of monopolizing the SCS" under the unchanged China's "nine - dash line" claim. This challenged the political and security situation in the region, directly challenged the position of the US and its allies in the region, and increased the competition between the US and China. Recently, China's reclamation, expansion and construction actions at shoals in Spratly Islands have altered the status quo; seriously threatened the sovereignty and interests of the claimants. After completing the reclamation and construction of Islands, development of public services and greening of artificial islands in the Spratly Islands, China will let its citizens live here, creating a legal basis for its claims for exclusive economic zone or continental shelf in this water; forming exclusive economic zones and continental shelf overlapping with other countries' in the SCS. China has decisively insisted on the "*nine-dash line*" claim and made it a basis for its negotiations with other claimants on the SCS sovereignty; forced and controlled other claimant's activities, challenged the role of other major powers, especially the role of the US and its allies in the region. Assessing this concern, international researchers noted that "in Spratly Islands, China is the only country building artificial islands from the formerly submerged creatures, during construction process; it caused bad damage to ecosystems. When this was completed, it made it as a demonstration to its exclusive economic zone and established the Air Defence Identification Zone too, which is making the SCS situation tense.

Secondly, in terms of economics, competition and conflict in the SCS, this will directly and seriously affect economic activities in the region and challenge maritime and aviation security situation in the SCS, causing damages to the economic development of the region. With the advantage of occupying reefs, China will strengthen law enforcement forces and the standing naval forces in the SCS, and strongly prevent marine economic activities of the countries in the SCS, especially exploration and exploitation of oil and gas, and fisheries. It will also support the implementation of China's maritime economic activities, obstructing air, maritime routes and seriously challenging the operation of marine economic development of other countries in the region.

Thirdly, in terms of Defence and security, competition and conflict in the SCS, China is making the regional security environment always tense, complex, and dangerous. This has risks of collision and conflicts, especially military conflict between major powers and claimants, which seriously create threats to peace, stability, and development of the region. It is creating difficulties for the process of promoting Defence and security cooperation between countries inside and outside the SCS.

Consequences of competitions and conflicts in the SCS are very serious and have adverse effects on the fields of Defence-security, economics, foreign policy, and politics of countries inside and outside the region. This is challenging the management of the SCS situation. As for solution to this problem, the claimants should actively avoid conflicts, especially military conflicts. They should also actively develop efforts to handle the situation, and turn the competition into an opportunity to promote cooperation, and create a peaceful, stable environment in the region. Major powers, especially ones in the SCS, need to change their current political policy, promote cooperation with neighbouring countries, take into account their legitimate interests and common interests of the stakeholders, and aim at finding a peaceful solution based on international law, particularly the UN Convention on Law of the Sea of 1982.

Dynamics of Competition, Cooperation and Conflict in East China Sea: South Korean Perspectives

Captain (Navy) Sukjoon Yoon (Retd)

Introduction

Northeast Asian security is lingering to maritime conflicts and competitions between/among the maritime territorial claimants and disputants regarding to various focal issues.[1] Recent maritime activities in the East China Sea (ECS) by countries or parties involved in exercising their maritime sovereignty and jurisdictional rights are mainly countries which are involved in an intractable maritime dispute due to geographic circumstances, such as China and Japan. They have focused on the badly intertwined and intractable maritime competitions, cooperation and conflicts. The disputed parties or claimants are located in the littoral areas off the East China Sea.

One of the increasing maritime conflicts and confrontation is the disputed maritime territorial sovereignty issues and delimitation of maritime boundary and continental shelf in the ECS, which is the remains the Diaoyu/Senkaku Islands in the ECS between China and Japan. It is observed that these tensions between China and Japan during the last couple of years have increased hence, heightened maritime cooperation between parties and claimants in the ECS should be reinforced by the establishment. The prevailing disagreements, competitions and conflicts in the ECS would be mitigated or at last resolved by the common understanding of maritime cooperation through the language of the UNCLOS.[2]

South Korea is known as one of the legitimate middle-power nation, and this can be used by seeking South Korea's constructive role in bridging the gap between the disputants and claimants in the disputed waters in the ECS. The ECS is covering most of the geographic locations including the area of the Jeju Islands of the Republic of Korea down up to the Bashi Straits and Pormosa straits between Taiwan and China.

In this sense, South Korea would be the 3rd party, and as its maritime-oriented policy and national security strategy is actively implemented, South Korea can provide some lessons and the best practices of establishing maritime cooperation, to its neighbouring countries such as China and Japan which are under maritime territorial disputes with each other. In part, the South Korea-China maritime cooperation is progressing better than expected or planned, and it would be the best practice to show the regional disputants and claimants as to how to cope with the maritime deficits and mitigate the disagreements between/among the entities.

It is fair to say that maritime territorial dispute in the ECS should be set aside, and more strategic trust amongst the disputants and claimants should be established. The approach of only wining the competing maritime sovereignty and jurisdictional rights by all means, including the unilateral interpretations of the UNCLOS and more assertive action than one of the competitors is reducing their live-or-die or win-or-lose arguments and creating instability.

What a Difference a Decade Makes – Tensions Heating Up

Many maritime crises and conflicts have occurred in Northeast Asian Seas during the last decade: in the West Sea (aka the Yellow Sea), the ECS, the East Sea (Sea of Japan), and the upper area of the South China Sea (SCS). The significant challenges include:

First, the application of the United Nations Convention Law of the Sea (UNCLOS) remains largely ineffective, as there is no agreement on the relevant maritime boundaries between neighbouring nations. So instead of drawing maritime boundaries based on principles of equitability, alternative legal principles and international laws, the issue such as historical rights, geographic situation and economic interactions, have taken precedence in claiming maritime jurisdiction. Countries in the Northeast Asia claimed their continental shelf, that extends far beyond what the UNCLOS has defined as the maximum of the coastal countries' right of declaring the Exclusive Economic Zone (EEZ).

Second, the rivalry between a rising maritime power and a declining naval power in the Northeast Asian Sea has impeded the development of comprehensive maritime cooperation mechanisms, which are so urgently needed to ensure maritime peace and stability. For instance, both the Japanese government's sudden registration of its national security act in September 2015 and the Chinese declaration in November 2013 that implemented its unilateral China's Air Defence Identification Zone (ADIZ) over the ECS can be understood as provocative actions, and nothing is being done to restrain such moves.[3]

Third, there is a growing trend of maritime nationalism, which originates in the domestic populism.[4] For instance, some of China's maritime claims in the ECS as "core national interests" seem to be nothing of the kind. Then there is the sudden Japanese nationalization of the Diaoyu/Senkaku Islands in September 2012, and also the renaming of some other islands in July 2014. And South Korea continues to insist on using both names for the eastern waters of the Korean Peninsula: East Sea (Sea of Japan), despite the International Hydrographic Organization's acknowledgement of the name "Sea of Japan" in recognition of Japan's contribution to surveying these waters during the 19th century.

Fourth, the disputed maritime areas have expanded, into the airspace above the high seas and underwater space below, with last November's declaration by the Chinese of an Air Defence Identification Zone in the ECS; and a further expansion into the underwater domain seems imminent, with all Northeast Asian navies moving to acquire sophisticated underwater platforms. Most notably North Korea is developing a new type of submarines with the capacity to launch ballistic missiles.[5] The potential battle space over the North Limit Line (NLL) between North Korea and South Korea in the West Sea already includes both the airspace above and the waters below the adjacent area: the Republic of Korea Ship (ROKS) *Cheonan* is believed to have been sunk by a North Korean submarine in 2010, and North Korean Unmanned Aerial Vehicles have been gathering covert intelligence since May 2014.

Lastly, to ensure their national maritime interests, upon which their economies depend, many nations in Northeast Asia are enhancing their maritime security forces capabilities in the disputed waters by pursuing modernization. Priority has been given to building larger surface vessels and submarines – China and Japan are acquiring organic air arms based on *quasi*-aircraft carrier-capability – and are establishing Marine Corps and modernizing their Coast Guard. Both policies are intended to provide maritime forces with a more power-based maritime security character, and the navies of the region are increasingly competitive. China and Japan are also apparently planning to establish new maritime security force units and command and control centers.

What Has Done in the East China Sea?

In the ECS, the Diaoyu/Senkaku Islands dispute can represent maritime competitions and conflicts, but maritime cooperation based on the strategic trust, operational confidence and tactical non-confrontation attitudes has not happened due to the prejudices and deficit, due to lacks of common understanding for using the seas. This has been a major obstacle to the development of amicable maritime partnerships between the coastal countries in the Northeast Asia, since the end of the Cold War.

These tensions are seen in the Diaoyu/Senkaku Islands disputes in the ECS between China and Japan. There are several infamous factors to be identified.

First, historical legacies are still lingering for the disputes. The Islands of the Diaoyu/Senkaku Islands were controlled by Japan from 1895 until 1945, after which they became the subject of the United States Civil Administration of the Ryukyu (Senkaku) Islands until 1972. The Islands were then returned to Japan under the Okinawa Revision Treaty, despite the fact that both China and Japan raised sovereignty claims over them before the UN Security Council in that year. That has caused fundamental problems between China and Japan of how to resolve the disputes. In July 2012, Japanese Prime Minister Yoshihiko Noda announced that the Japanese government would purchase and nationalize the islands and current Shinzo Abe administration decided to rename all islands of the Diaoyu/Senkaku Islands in 2014. These actions fueled more fire on the intractable disputes in the ECS.

Second, deep prejudices and mistrust between/among the coastal countries as to how to apply the international laws and legal principles like the UNCLOS to the disputed waters have disrupted the intentions or efforts to coordinate the differences and disagreements. From the 1970s until the early 1990s there was a tacit understanding between both countries to keep the dispute under wraps as they pursued diplomatic rapprochement and economic development. However, the Japanese government explicitly denied such an understanding in the 2010 and 2012 crises. The activities of Chinese naval and air forces have increased since 2012. According to Japan, the number of Chinese vessels entering the waters around the islands has jumped from around zero per month before September 2012 to upwards of 28 percent per month since. The Japanese costal guard has enhanced its activities and capabilities accordingly.

Third, all wanted to rely upon more power-based resolution, rather than rule-based maritime cooperation. In December 2008 two vessels from the China Maritime Surveillance (CMS) force entered the maritime territorial waters around the islands in an apparent bid to scuttle a gas field agreement between Japan and China. This was the first time that Chinese government ships had entered what Japan views as its maritime sovereignty, and its maritime territorial waters. In September 2010 the Japanese coast guard arrested the captain of a Chinese trawler after the latter collided with two Japanese patrol vessels in the disputed waters near the islands. Between 2011 and 2012, on three occasions, Chinese government ships entered these waters: in August 2011 (two vessels' from the Bureau of Fisheries Administration), March 2012 (one CMS vessel) and July 2012 (three vessels from the Bureau of Fisheries Administration).

Fourth, there are vicious action-reaction cycles between claimants and disputants. In September 2012 – December 2013, Chinese vessels entered the maritime territorial waters around the islands 74 times and maintained a near-continuous presence in the contiguous zone just beyond the maritime territorial boundary. Military activities escalated on both sides, including: the locking of weapons-targeting radar on 30 January 2013 by a Chinese frigate on to a Japanese destroyer, the crew of which went to battle stations; the movement of Chinese ballistic missiles closer to the coast; the use of Chinese drones; and large-scale naval training exercises by China. Unfortunately, this caused the third party's involvement on the ECS issues. For instance, the US sent two B-52 bombers flying into the newly declared Chinese ADIZs in November 2013 and Chinese reaction has been more absolute and confrontational.

Fifth, operational maritime crisis management system should be established albeit more high-profile political decision makers' agree for political solutions, emphasizing common interest, and not self-interest. In November 2014, the Chinese President Xi Jinping and Japanese Prime Minister Shinzo Abe met at the APEC Summit in Beijing for their first formal talks since 2012. Despite this agreement, there are still many things required in conducting the operational procedures of establishing the hotlines between the operational maritime security forces units in China and Japan. In contrast, China and South Korea had established their bilateral operational naval hotline between the two navies' subordinated units in 2013.

What Policy Options for Maritime Cooperation?

From the South Korean perspective, there are several comprehensive suggestions for mitigating tense standoff between China and Japan in the ECS. These can be regarded as general principles which can help to mitigate the emerging threats and challenges occurring in the East China Sea to the Northeast Asian maritime security.

First, maritime confidence building and crisis management measure requires an iterative process of strategic-political dialogue to overcome the outdated perspectives and attendant barriers to cooperation which linger on in the decision-making chains.[6] Before effective and stable regional maritime security can be established, which involves maritime confidence-building, the region needs some mechanisms of stipulating the maritime crisis management system to prevent crises and conflicts from happening. For example, in July 2013, China and Japan agreed to establish a hotline between their highest military authorities, and between the very military institutions which bear the primary responsibility for determining security policy and for implementing maritime security strategies. In November 2014 during the just stop-by bilateral summit between China and Japan the two governments agreed to establish operational hotlines between the two maritime security force units, but the process is still undergoing without substantial development between China and Japan.

Second, the third party including US which appear to have a great deal of interest, intelligence collecting operations in the airspace above or the waters beneath disputed areas are potentially very disruptive.[7] In particular, any involvement of third party assets in these activities, such as drones equipped with long-range sensors and weapons will likely lead to intractable misunderstandings. Thus, to avoid maritime crises being triggered in this way, the nations of the Northeast Asian region should develop protocols for prior notification of intelligence-related activities above and beneath the disputed waters. The clashes between the Chinese maritime law enforcement forces and USN oceanic surveying ships in 2008, 2013 and 2014 are the examples of the third party's involvement on the bilateral maritime disputes of the ECS.

Third, maritime security is best served by all nations implementing their aims with the lowest possible level of force. Maritime security should not be a military issue, but more like a constabulary task in which navies play a diplomatic role: thus, any confrontations between disputing parties should focus on law enforcement and maintaining good order at sea. In this way, through predictability and transparency, the nations of the Northeast Asian region should resolve to establish a safer maritime domain for all, and to create the conditions for a region without military purpose.

South Korea's Role as an Impartial Middle-Power

What the ECS dispute actually needs is a dilution of the intractable antagonistic power politics, to allow the involvement of constructive middle powers,who are major stakeholders in the preservation of regional peace and stability and can bring a fresh perspective.

South Korea's economy is absolutely dependent on sea-based trade, and the country also imports much of its energy needs by sea. Indeed, the seas are so vital to South Korea's peace and prosperity that maritime strategy is central to the national interest: the country can fairly be characterized as "Maritime South Korea". South Korea is a major player in the regional economy, abides strictly by international legal regimes, and is a genuine middle power. Surely it deserves a greater voice in representing the common interests of the region, in particular on the intractable ECS issues.

If new security structures are to be established for the Indo-Asia-Pacific region, they must take account of the interests of all the surrounding nations, not just of China and the US. New ideas are needed and South Korea, together with other middle powers, must be involved.

From the South Korean perspective, any such framework should take account of several essential propositions: first, the ECS crisis must be urgently addressed, to prevent further deterioration; second, any proposals suggested must be acceptable to China and Japan; third, all points of disagreement should be resolved through a legal process according to established international practices – insisting upon opaque historical references, such as the nine-dashed line, is unhelpful.[8]

Opinion in South Korea, among policy-makers, scholars, experts on the national security affairs and businesspeople, is supportive of continuing expansion of trade and investment links with China and Japan, anticipating significant benefits from China's ambitious BRI project and Korea-Japan maritime security cooperation, but we are seriously concerned about the accumulating problems in the ECS over the past few years.

In this regard, ECS tensions cannot be allowed to interfere with freedom of navigation on the high seas or EEZ because all the regional economies depend on maritime transit. This is clearly a common interest. Some have even argued that China is effectively a free rider since the freedom of navigation it enjoys in the region depends on the US. Several main themes have emerged from discussions in the South Korean media and academics forums: First, tensions and clashes between China and Japan are mainly attributable to the regional maritime instability and disorder. China and Japan as the world's second- and third-largest economies respectively accounted for US$ 2.9 trillion worth of goods experts in 2013, much of which was shipped through the East China Sea. Conflict between the two countries could bring to a standstill six of the world's largest ports responsible for half of all container traffic.[9] South Korea should be one of the regional stakeholders concerning about the Possible conflicts between China and Japan in the East China Sea.

The vicious cycles of action and reaction involving China and Japan are becoming ever more dangerous and deadly. Fourth, the most serious problem is China's efforts to eventually wrest control of the whole ECS, despite US determination to remain the dominant regional maritime power.

In the short term, China and Japan will continue to compete for control of the ECS, and so continuing tensions are inevitable, but actually both sides, have an interest in maintaining the uneasy status quo, and at the day-to-day level of interaction they are mostly concerned with preserving face. The long term is another story: so long as the ECS remains in dispute, the risks of confrontation will grow. If China becomes stronger, it will grow confident enough to test the resolve of its neighbour and rival, Japan. If China becomes weaker, it will look to territorial conflicts as a cautious way to rally public support.

However things turn out, South Korea will find a major role in facilitating negotiations between China and Japan: infact all the stakeholders of the wider region should be involved in resolving the future of the ECS. South Korea, as an impartial middle power, articulates priorities which reflect the common interests of the region as a whole:

(1) preserving freedom of navigation on the high seas, (2) ensuring free trade among the nations of the region and between them and the rest of the world, (3) upholding the universal principles of the generally agreed international legal system.

In September 2013, the South Korean government released a strategy document outlining its intention to play a leadership role in fostering multinational cooperation: this "Northeast Asia Peace Initiative" is based on strategic cooperation against nontraditional threats, including regional maritime issues.[10] "Maritime South Korea" is an important stakeholder in the security of the region, and as an established middle power is now planning to implement "open seas protection", which means that the South Korean navy and maritime enforcement agencies will expand their offshore security operations, especially targeting North Korean military provocations in the seas around the Korean Peninsula.

Conclusion

Over the last six years, the ECS has become a seething cauldron which could explode at any time. China continues its claim based on historical evidences and Westphalian perception of land projection, Japan merely grumbles and relies on US-Japan Defence treaty as the US President Barack Obama's proclamation of being Diaoyu/Senkaku Islands part of the obligations of the bilateral Defence treaty. Only the legitimatizing of the ECS issue may offer any prospect of stabilizing the region: the middle powers must become involved in negotiating a new regional security architecture which allows sustainable peace and good order to facilitate the economic interactions which are the common interest of all parties. South Korea is a close security partner with Japan, but also a strategic cooperative partner of China; it respects international law, and is a member of the UNCLOS, but is not involved in any territorial disputes in the ECS. No country is better placed to initiate a debate on opening up ECS issues to encompass many more voices than just those of China and Japan.

Endnotes

1   Kun-Chin Lin and Andres VillarGertner, *Maritime Security in the Asia-Pacific: China and the Emerging Order in the East and South China Seas* (London: The Royal Institute of International Affairs, July 2015), pp. 5-8.

2   Reinhard Drift, "The Japan-China Confrontation Over the Senkaku/Diaoyu Islands – Between "shelving" and "dispute escalation,"*Asia-Pacific Journal*, Vol. 12, Issue 30, No. 3.

3   Michael Machael McDevitt, "Will China Refashion the Asian Maritime Order?" Strategy 21, Vol. 17, No. 1, Winter 2014, pp. 202-221.

4   Ramses Amer, "China and South China Sea: How to Manage Maritime Crisis," Strategy 21, Vol. 17, No. 1, Winter, 2014, pp. 222-252; You Ji, Policy Brief: Deciphering Beijing's Maritime Security Policy and Strategy in Managing Sovereignty Disputes in the China Seas (Singapore: S. Rajaratnam School of International Studies, October 2013)

5   Shin Hyon-hee, "N.K. Launched ballistic missile submarine,"*The Korea Herald*, November 3, 2014, p. 1.

6   Sam Bateman, "Maritime confidence building measures – an overview," in *Discussion Papers for Maritime Confidence Building Measures in the South China Sea Conference*, InterContinental Hotel, Sydney, 11-13 August 2013 (Sydney: Australian Strategic Policy Institute, 2013).

7   Robert Sutter, "Rebalancing, China and Asian Dynamics - Obama's Good Fit," *PacNet*, #1 Monday, January 6, 2014.

8   See *IHS Jane's Defence Weekly*, 18 February 2015, p. 24. Map shows a comparison of China's dashed-line claims made in 1947 and 2009.

9   Kun-Chin Lin and Andres VillarGertner, Maritime Security in the Asia-Pacific: China and the Emerging Order in the East and South China Seas, p. 8.

10 See MOFA, *Northeast Asia Peace and Cooperation Initiative: 2015* (Seoul: Ministry of Foreign Affairs, 2015).

Interplay between Security of the IOR and Dynamics in South China Sea

Dr. Huang Yunsong

Introduction

Emerging powers are expanding their presence into the regions that they previously were not familiar with; this usually attracts concerns and doubts. With the rapidly growing economic ties in the Indian Ocean Region, and also the war ships and submarines randomly cruising since 2008, China's intention for this specific area has been seriously questioned by a few littoral and extra regional states. My observation on the issue is as follows:

China's Presence in the Indian Ocean Region

Firstly, China's presence in the Indian Ocean Region is benign in nature, and closely connected to its overseas economic efforts. Taking Chinese-African trade relations for example, with the bilateral trade soaring to over $200 billion and its direct investment in Africa increasing by nearly 50 percent annually, China has become the largest trading partner of the poorest continent since 2009. Hoping to keep the momentum in developing the economic ties with Africa, and other states in the IOR, China has committed itself to its infrastructural up-gradation along the maritime trade route, by bringing in investments in port facilities in a number of IOR states, and exploring opportunities in Maldives, the Seychelles, and Mauritius.

In its overseas economic initiative, China regards India is as a major partner. China–India bilateral trade was over $70 billion in 2014, and the greater potential is yet to be realised. Undoubtedly, a friendly bilateral relation with India has become one of the most important pillars of China's foreign policy. Talking about the economic prospects between China and India, I am obliged to share with you an interesting conversation that I had with an Indian businessman on the flight to New Delhi. He is a fairly successful one, driving a Mercedes and spending nearly $8000 on household monthly, used to shuttle between New Delhi and Guangzhou quite often. When I mentioned to him about the 70 billion bilateral trade, he insisted that I was fooled by the official statistics. He told me that most Indian companies has chosen to hide up to 90 percent of their business transaction with their Chinese partners for tax evasion, and the practice will continue to be prevalent if the India Government does not lower the tax rate. According to him, the trade between China and India should be at least 10 times bigger. This may be bragging, but cannot be entirely wrong. At least it will be right to speculate that, at the economic front, China and India are considerably more reliant on each other than our recognition, which makes a solid basis for peace and prosperity in the IOR.

Unfortunately, China's economic initiatives have been seriously misinterpreted by the strategic communities in India, saying it is economic means for military ends. It is more realistic, in my opinion, to describe it as economic ends through limited military means.

Secondly, China's naval presence is marginal and capable of no threat to the IOR. The Chinese naval presence in the Indian Ocean, especially in the Arabian Sea, is not even commensurate to its huge economic and strategic interests in place. Our naval strength is and will continue to be bound in the South and East China Sea, focusing on defending sovereignty rights over Taiwan, the Diaoyu islands, and the maritime interests related to certain land features.

The strongest foreign military presence in the IOR is maintained by the US. The Indian Ocean is the operating area of its 5th, 6th and 7th fleets. The 5th, reactivated in 1995, is a fully Indian Ocean fleet, and comprised of a carrier strike group, amphibious ready group, and a number of other ships and aircrafts, with 15,000 personnel serving afloat and 1,000 ashore. In addition, there are around 5,000 troops living in the US military base on Diego Garcia.

Except for its supremacy in the Arabian Sea and the Bay of Bengal, India has also nurtured its military presence in at least 8 foreign states, including the surveillance installations in Madagascar, Mauritius and Seychelles, capable of exercising meaningful influence over various choke points around the Indian Ocean to secure the sea lanes, especially the Strait of Malacca.

Since December 2008, with the authorization from the UN Security Council, China has dispatched 21 Escort Task Groups to the Indian Ocean to repress piracy and respond to humanitarian crisis in the region. In addition to counter-piracy patrols, the Task Groups also conducted missions to escort cargo ships carrying chemical weapons out Syria, and provide search and rescue support for Malaysia Airlines MH370.

Among these 63 Chinese naval ships of the task groups, half of them belong to the South Sea Fleet, and the total number of the sailors in each Task Group is usually around 800. Has anyone asked the question, why South Sea Fleet? The purpose of its heavy involvement in the missions is to avail them the training opportunities for low intensity combat proficiency, an obvious response to the tensions in South China Sea.

Thirdly, China's naval presence is on ad hoc basis. As Chinese military experts pointing out, China's Escort Task Groups operating in the Indian Ocean are very different from a regular naval deployment, and legitimacy of their operation largely relies on the renewal of the relevant UNSC resolution. In other words, there must be some very good reasons, if Chinese navy decides to stay in the Indian Ocean when the threat from piracy and terrorism is no more.

The thriller stories of Chinese ghost fleet and the String of Pearls, focusing on China's military appetite in the Indian Ocean, have been developed into something unreal, without the least respect for the fact that there is almost no diplomatically reliable, logistically functional and militarily defendable strategic foothold for China's naval force in this region.

Since the low level presence of Chinese navy in the IOR works perfectly well to keep our cargo ships and tankers free of pirate harassment, and guarantees that the chance of escalated confrontation held in check, there is no necessity for China to resort to a regular naval deployment in the near future.

Similarly, the so called string of pearls consisting of multiple naval bases along the rim of the Indian Ocean is not only too luxurious for China to afford, but also incompatible to China's capability and aspiration. This is why Chinese strategic communities usually take this hypothesis as a joke. It is true that Chinese government has funded the majority of the $1.2 billion construction in Gwadar, but independent media such as Economist has found the port facility project to be commercial in nature. The berth rights and logistic support possibly available to China's naval vessels doesn't automatically turn Gwadar into a military base comparable to Diego Garcia.

Fourthly, China is in favor of a collective security mechanism in the Indian Ocean Region, which is supposed to be inclusive to all stakeholders. China's security concept does not support division of spheres of influence, or advocate for the notions such as strategic backyard. For the past three decades, this security concept has influenced China's foreign policies very deeply, and helped in achieving better relations with ASEAN, formation of the SCO, and the joint efforts with the U.S. in control of nuclear proliferation in North Korea and Iran.

In order to secure its oversea interests, China has to be pragmatic enough to depend on various collective security mechanisms around the world. This established approach pursued by China allows little room for hegemon or monopoly on security matters in specific regions. It is also true that foreign military bases are not prerequisite for the collective security mechanism to work.

More intriguingly, in regard to India's renewed enthusiasm in promoting the Indian Ocean as a Zone of Peace, I believe that Beijing will stand firmly for New Delhi, if the suggestion of no military bases in the IOR is for all the major powers including the US. I would also like to mention that during the Adhoc Committee meeting in July 2005, the Chinese representative did call for the major powers outside the region to eliminate their military bases in the IOR.

When security of the IOR comes into question, we sincerely encourage the relevant parties to consider and respect China's well-grounded concern for the safety of its economic activities and crucial trading routes, by assuming an objective attitude in telling the difference between presence and threat, the distinction between commercial ports and military bases. China is willing and capable of being a net provider of security to the IOR, as long as it is not excluded from the collective security mechanism yet to emerge.

Dynamics in the South China Sea

Sea lines of communication are so indispensable and important to national security and prosperity of all states, that any attempts to disrupt international shipping lanes should not be tolerated by the world community. Chinese government has reiterated at various international forums its position on safeguarding and ensuring freedom of navigation and over flight throughout the region, especially in the South China Sea. Over 100,000 vessels sail through the South China Sea every year, their freedom of navigation has not been interrupted. For almost half of India's external trade that passes through the South China Sea, there has never been any issue with the freedom of navigation. In my opinion, the freedom of navigation being endangered in the South China Sea is actually a pseudo-proposition, and is not the key issue in the South China Sea.

Because of the cruise by the US naval destroyer Lassen within 12 nautical miles of Subi Reef（渚碧岛）and the US bombers closely flying by, the situation in the South China Sea is seemingly approaching to a breaking point. The cruise and over flight was perceived by Chinese government as escalatory and provocative, because they were meant to exert undue pressure on China alone, and encourage the relevant states to take a tougher stance in negotiations for solution. When China is fully aware that these activities around its artificial islands are not in violation of international law, it has become pointless and counter-productive for the US or its intimate partner states to carry on with the operation. It's unwise for the US to be obsessed with threat of force when dealing with China, if it really wants both parties to have enough room to maneuver.

Since India, along with a few other states, has publicly voiced its support for freedom of navigation in international waters, including the South China Sea, we really need to focus our attention on the different interpretation of UNCLOS concerning the freedom of navigation. After careful examination of relevant legal documents, I found that India's perception of the freedom of navigation is virtually very similar to that of China, which rules out the foreign military activities in its exclusive economic zone. As per the Declaration made upon ratification of UNCLOS by India on June 29, 1995, the second paragraph reads as this, "The Government of the Republic of India understands that the provisions of the Convention do not authorize other States to carry out in the exclusive economic zone and on the continental shelf military exercises or maneuvers, in particular those involving the use of weapons or explosives without the consent of the coastal State."

In addition to China and India, another 26 states (including Vietnam) have also put restrictions on foreign military activities according to their interpretation of the UNCLOS. In this sense, international law (including the UNCLOS) does not provide the United States with the navigational freedom as it claims. The other thing that needs to be stressed is that the UNCLOS doesn't prohibit signatory parties from the activities of land reclamation. If the US wants to play judge on whether China, Vietnam or Philippine has been excessive in land reclamation and claiming maritime interests, please earn the ticket by ratifying the UNCLOS first. Because the UNCLOS is not simply a forum for any bystanders, but a legal regime for parties committed to it.

In all, the confrontation between the U.S. and China in the South China Sea, which, is not going to be developed into conflicts soon, actually has little to do with the international law. It is more like a US strategic maneuver to defuse its competitor, and the international law happens to be one of its handy tools.

The Six-Point Proposal on the Diaoyu Islands

Compared to the South China Sea, the dispute between China and Japan on the Diaoyu Islands seems to be less complicated. China's hard-line position on the Diaoyu islands was largely caused by Japan's aggressive denial of the dispute and the unilateral action to nationalize its control over the islands in 2012. Japan's rejection to recognize China's control over the islands prior to 1895, and the binding effects of the Potsdam Declaration upon the islands makes it no longer flexible to re-acknowledge the dispute, let alone to compromise for an endurable solution.

To my surprise, the U.S. has already put forward a constructive proposal through proper channel to China as an interim solution to the dispute. This six-point proposal is indeed very important, partially consistent with China's suggestion to shelve the dispute, and reasonably worthy of a serious consideration.

First, neither party should contest the right of the other to claim the sovereignty over the Diaoyu Islands; second, China should agree that Japan maintains administrative jurisdiction over the Diaoyu Islands; third, Japan gives consent to transfer of the right to use the Diaoyu Islands to a Joint Committee, which features an equal number of representatives from both countries and the rotation of presidency, overseeing issues such as scientific surveys and tourism development; fourth, both parties promise to put an end to the unilateral maritime patrol around or aerial patrol over the Diaoyu Islands, and any patrol within 12 NM should be jointly carried out on the basis of consensus. The Diaoyu islands will be managed by the Joint Committee and only be open for non-military purposes such as ecotourism; fifth, both parties should agree to separate the issue of the Diaoyu Islands from other disputes over territory and sovereignty in the West Pacific, in other words, the law of the sea will not be applicable to the Diaoyu islands; sixth, both parties should agree to refrain from new disputes over any other islands in the West Pacific.

China welcomes the constructive spirit that the US proposal contains and keeps an open mind to the same. However, a substantial bilateral discussion between China and Japan over a solution, either interim or endurable, largely depends on Japan's acceptance of the 1972 agreement to set aside the islands dispute by revoking the decision to nationalize the Diaoyu Islands. Unfortunately, China's patience towards Shinzo Abe's right-wing administration has drastically worn out, and it is becoming less likely for Beijing to acquiesce the second point of the proposal, that is Japan's administrative jurisdiction over the islands. Considering Abe's determination to interfere with the South China Sea, which could further complicate the situation in the East China Sea, the chance for China to narrow its difference with Japan may become even smaller.

Conclusion

95 percent of India's total external trade and over 70 percent of its oil imports transit the maritime domain. In China's case, 90 percent of its foreign trade and 95 percent of its oil imports relies on maritime shipping lanes. To summarize, China and India shares common concerns and common interests in terms of their reliance on the maritime security in the seven seas as a whole. Any strategic decision detrimental to the maritime interests of the other party has a risk of backfire, because no state in the world can guarantee its maritime route will remain untouched when sabotaging the others.

Taiwan-China Relations: Risk or Opportunity for the Peace of East Asia

Dr. Chi-shin Chang

Introduction

From 1949 to now, Taiwan-China relations, also known as 'Cross-strait relations' have been very unique, as well controversial, issues to both the researchers and practitioners in international relations.[1] In his National-Day speech, President Ma Ying-jeou spent more than one-third of the time and laid out his efforts on promoting cross-strait relations, it shows how the leader in Taiwan cares about this issue.

To the whole world's surprise, on November 5th, President Ma publicly announced he'll meet President Xi jin-ping on November 7th in Singapore while Xi is in the state visit there.[2] Though it seems to arouse world emotion and stimulate excitement in public, those locals who were against Ma soon ran to the President's Office and protested this under-the-table meeting; one of the civil organizations even went to the court and sued Ma for committing treason. Indeed, in term of history, there're not so many cases a President of the country among all these East Asian ones, (from his first -- until the last -- term as president), would have this kind of policy preference which is obviously tilting towards China.

This paper entitled as 'Taiwan-China Relations: Risk or Opportunity for the Peace of East Asia?' will be divided into three parts. First, a brief review of past cross-strait relations will be presented. Secondly, the policies of the ruling Kuomintang (KMT), especially when Ma assumed the position as President from 2008 to 2016, also with its impacts on cross-strait relations, will be further analyzed. In the author's view, Ma's strategies, with the ruling Party's policies toward China, are the main factors that create the most difficult challenges that Taiwan is forced to face and the risks, not exactly opportunities, for both China and Taiwan. Last but not least would be the implications for East Asia. There are risks if Taiwan is pushed close to China, because the KMT shall then directly/indirectly give legitimacy to China's moves, and empowers it to claim sovereignty with assertiveness over the East and South China sea. Under this situation, the other Great Powers, especially the US, would not tolerate and be silent about the situation tilts over China, then expected and unexpected conflict might just happen in a sudden way which would then endanger this region.

Endless Power Struggle between Taiwan and China

The current situation in the Taiwan Strait is basically evolved from the result of power struggles between the Nationalist Party (Kuomintang, AKA KMT) and the Chinese Communist Party (CCP, or Communist Party in China, CPC). Compare it with the situation before 1949, the main difference is that there's now a great fault line, tremendous water with width ranges from 130km to 410km, separates these two parties and creates a huge 'buffer zone'. The struggle continues without doubts, since they're still looking forward to both legitimacy and final unification of the two lands, Mainland China and Taiwan. To understand the current situation, we need to avoid retrospection of the past history. According to the experts, there are three phases of relationship between China and Taiwan that evolved from 1949 to now: A Military confrontation, 1949-1958 after CCP defeated KMT and took the Mainland in 1949, CCP insisted of using force to destroy and occupy places those KMT stayed in. Both sides of the Taiwan Strait is still haunted by the shadow of war. At least four battles -- including Battle of Guningtou (古寧頭) in 1949, the First Battle of Quemoy (金門) in 1954, Battle of Dachen Archipelago (大陳島) in 1955, Battle of Yijiangshan Islands (一江山) in 1955, and the Second Battle of Quemoy (八二三砲戰) in 1958 -- happened during this period. From a constructivist view,

Taiwan and China takes each other as a real enemy without any chance to compromise.[3] Under that condition, military confrontation lasted for at least 10 years. The catalysts for the next peaceful period were the two events, including China joined with 29 African and Asian states and held the first Asian-African Conference in Bandung, Indonesia, in which China promised to be more peace-oriented, stressed 'Five Principles of Peaceful Coexistence'.[4] During the meeting, Premier Zhou En-lai claimed, for the first time, the possibility to liberate Taiwan with peaceful measures. On other hand, China also began the ambassador-level dialogue with the US in the same year. Based on that, China reoriented its policy toward Taiwan and gave up the position to solve 'Taiwan Problem' with military force.

Legitimacy Struggle, 1959-1978

The main theme of this period is the struggle for legitimacy between Taiwan and China, AKA 'hanzeibuliang li' (漢賊不兩立), especially characterized by the struggle for the UN membership and the seat at the Security Council. China pushed hard for its own membership and replacement of Taiwan in UN with strenuous efforts. However, under strong support from the US, Taiwan kept enjoying the legitimate status, not only in the UN and the other important international governmental organizations, but also of being the only legal representative of 'China'. Until the Vietnamese communist party turned the tides of Vietnam War, US never stopped its position on Taiwan's favorable status. For keeping this legitimacy, the leader of Taiwan, Generalissimo Chiang Kai-shek, insisted of breaking diplomatic ties with those who recognize the New Communist regime in Mainland China as legal. Taiwan was finally expelled from UN and the other important international organisations (IOs). At the same time, quite a bit of countries broke their ties with Taiwan and established diplomatic relationship with China.

Peaceful confrontation, 1979-1987

The struggle for legitimacy really ended in December 15, 1978, followed US's recognition of the People Republic of China (PRC). In the beginning of next year, PRC began to soften its stance and announced

'*A Message to Compatriots in Taiwan*' (告台灣同胞書) in 1ˢᵗ January, stressed 'Peaceful Unification' by promoting 'Three Links'(三通) and 'Four exchanges'(四流) [5] Three years later, Chairman Deng Xiao-ping released and further elaborated his 'One Country Two Systems' (一國兩制) as the peaceful grounding for unification. One of the main reasons for China to do so is that China was eager to have closer economic relations with US and attract more investment. China believed that this will earn good image from US if it showed goodwill towards Taiwan. Another important reason is that China felt the opportunities to unite with Taiwan are diminishing following the aging, or even death, of those old KMT leaders in Taiwan. As for Taiwan, the son of Chiang Kai-shek, President Chiang Ching-kuo, decided to execute 'Three Noes'(三不) and 'Unification under Three Principles of the People'(三民主義統一中國) to counter and weaken the reactive force triggered by PRC propaganda.[6] In any terms, no more gun smokes could be smelled during this period, economic development is the common goal for them to pursue. However, a Taiwanese pilot hijacked a China Airline cargo airplane in 1986, which forced the officials of the two sides to meet and negotiate for a solution. This accident dramatically ended so called 'Three-Nos' policy and inevitably highlighted the complicated and changing nature of cross-strait relations. KMT, still the ruling part, formally lifted martial law. Cross-Strait relations hereafter began to undergo a transformation.

Detent and Reconciliation, 1988-1999

After Chiang's death in 1988, Lee Teng-hui, the Vice President to Chiang, stepped up and became the President. Facing more and more close cross-strait interactions and exchanges, Lee pragmatically promoted democratic reforms in domestic, at the same time; he began his full-fledged plan on promoting cross-strait relations. First, he pushed to adopt the Guideline of National Unification (國統綱領) in March, 1991; created a non-governmental organization, Strait Exchange Foundation (SEF)[7]. In the same month; declared termination of the Period of Communist Rebellion in May, 1991, and last but not least, recognized PRC as a legitimate regime. All these institutional changes pave the way for following talks in 1993, which saw the participation of SEF and its counterpart, Association for Relations Across the Taiwan Straits (ARATS). Before the talk, so called '1992 consensus' was taken into the pot.[8] One thing for sure is that both sides couldn't agree on the meaning of 'One China'. After the 1993 Singapore talk, Hong Kong and Macau were separately returned to China in 1997 and 1999, which consolidated the foundation and were used by China as two role models of 'One Country Two Systems'. However, at least three events happened in the last half of 1990s deteriorated and alienated each other again:

a.   1995 - Lee accepted invitation and visited the Cornell University;

b.   1996 - China launched ballistic missiles, also conducted a series of military exercises, targeted at Taiwan, which was known as 'The Second Crisis of Taiwan Strait'; for preventing the dangers, US dispatched two Carrier battle groups to cruise around Taiwan strait;

c   1999 – Lee was interviewed by Germany media and defined cross-Strait relations as 'a special State-to-State relationship' (the two-state theory), which seriously irritated China.

Ideological Stalemate without Official Exchanges, 2000-2007

From 2000-2008, Taiwan is in a situation different from those years when KMT dominated this island. In 2000, the opposition political party which prefers independence of Taiwan, Democratic Progressive Party (DPP, AKA 'Green'), defeated KMT and won the presidential election. This is the first time that political parties in Taiwan can transfer political power in peace. DPP's candidate, Chen Shui-bian, became the new President. To show his good will in handling with cross-Strait relations, President Chen formerly pledged 'Four Noes and One without' (四不一沒有) in his inaugural speech.[9] He reiterated 'integration theory' in the 2001 New Year Speech and claimed that 'Both sides of the Taiwan Strait can start by integrating their economies through trade and cultural exchanges;'[10] He even approved 'Three Small Links' (小三通) in Quemoy, Matsu, Mawei (Fujian) in the same year; charter flights between Taiwan and China also came to reality in 2003.

However, ideological differences between DPP and CCP seem to be more than those between KMT and CCP, and are too difficult to overcome. President Chen, also with his DPP colleagues, denied recognizing 'One China Principle' or '1992 consensuses', or taking them as the prerequisite for any possible talks. In China's view, Chen is unpredictable and of course deserves no trust for his 'Green' background. And to China's surprise, President Chen threw out the concept of 'One Country on Each Side' on 3rd August 2002, in a telecast to the annual conference of the World Federation of Taiwanese Association. Besides that, he called for a referendum on Taiwan's future. All these moves soon seriously infuriates China. All the official exchanges channels were cut off in the following years. However, under DPP's rule, Taiwan kept its pace to further democratization and localization. With these driving forces behind, plus the consistent military and political intimidation from China, the people in Taiwan gradually changed their national identity from 'Republic of China' to 'Republic of China on Taiwan', even to 'Taiwan', in that case, more and more people on this island identify themselves as 'Taiwanese', not 'Chinese'.

China took it for granted that President Chen will keep changing the status-quo in his second term, one of its political measures to restraint Chen is pass the 'Anti-Secession Law' in 2005. To counter that, President Chen took a 'skillful' step to scrap the National Unification Council and the Guidelines for National Unifications and clearly broke the 'one without' principle. This certainly made China angry, and at the same time, Taiwan also paid off for making US-Taiwan relations restrained.[11] There's one thing which should be specifically noted is that even though both sides stopped political exchange, however; their economic ties strengthened and doubled during this period.

Taiwan's Policy towards China under Ma Ying-jeou's Regime

KMT's Chairman, Ma Ying-jeou, successfully won the 2008 Presidential Election and took regime back in 2000. When Compared with his predecessor, Ma is apparently against the idea to push Taiwan to become an independent state, on the contrary, he is strongly intended to shorten the gap between Taiwan and China. He takes himself as one of the

'Chinese'(中華民族), not a 'Taiwanese'. In such a case, the relationship between Taiwan and China were bound to improve, when President Ma became the President. He further defines what he did to bring both sides closer than ever is to create a kind of 'status-quo'. Cross-strait relations, no matter in which side it is view is now experiencing an all-time high. China accordingly appears to have eased its attitude in dealing with 'Taiwan affairs'.

However, what we can take from the Chinese history is that, China would certainly not be satisfied by that 'status-quo', but will hope to reunite with Taiwan and hit the mark of 'One China'. Accordingly, the author took it for granted that President Ma is actually playing 'balance-ball-tilt-over' game on the edge. One more step, he might not just put Taiwan's interest in jeopardy, but also bring shadow of war to East Asia. President Ma's policy toward China could be further analyzed as below:

Grand Strategy of 'Rapprochement with China, Ally with the US and be friend with Japan'

Before Ma won the election, he was for revising and making up the mistakes that former President Chen had made, President Ma believes that Taiwan should give up both attitude and strategies of confrontation. China and Taiwan both belong to 'One China', which is clearly defined by the Constitution of Republic of China.

Not just that, President Ma decides to pursue policy which will keep three Great Powers at arm's length, later labeled as a grand strategy composed of 'rapprochement with China, ally with the US and be friend with Japan'. This grand strategy obviously outlines three main goals:

a) Taiwan will firstly reconcile with China,

b) Second, in terms of security, Taiwan will stand by the US, and the last,

c) Make and keep Japan as a friend.

Though there's no concrete measures mentioned or supplemented by any government officials, however; President Ma believed that this strategy is the bedrock, to secure Taiwan's future. The then-Secretary General of the National Security Council, Su chi, prioritized this strategy with 'rapprochement with China' first, and defined this strategy as 'right and necessary', because 'Taiwan can't afford the price of isolating itself (鎖國)'. He also criticized those who were against this strategy and were beyond his understanding.[12] Under the guidance of this strategy, the government decided to take non-confrontational approach toward China and open the way for 'Viable Diplomacy (活路外交)' and 'Diplomatic Truce (外交休兵)'. In addition to that, on August 26th, 2008, during an interview by Mexican Media, President Ma took initiative and asserted that 'Cross-Strait relations are not state-to-state relations,' the relations at most are 'special relations'. On 10th October 2013, President Ma reiterated this and also restricting any other options and gave- definition of cross-strait relations in his National-Day speech. In a word, all these are nothing but tactics which evolved from the strategy of 'reconcile with China'.[13] These also signify that Ma's government changed its attitude toward cross-strait relations, which were very different from that of President Lee Teng-hui and Chen Shui-bian. It soon earned China's trust which totally matched with what China wanted from Taiwan.

1992 Consensus with 'Economic First, Politics Later'

As mentioned before, the '1992 Consensus' was supposed to be there in 1992. However, each side of the Taiwan Strait has its different interpretation. What China want is the first half, 'There's only one China'; however, what Taiwan want is the second half, 'each one has its own interpretation about one China'. Based on this 'agree to disagree' consensus, Ma's government decides to open dialogue with China and made up the gap with 'economic first, politics later' strategy.

China, especially under the new leadership -- including fourth-generation leader, Hu Jing-tao, and the fifth-generation leader, Xi Jin-ping -- changed their policies toward Taiwan, and is more willing to take aggressive united-front initiatives to deal with so-called 'Taiwan affairs'. Driven by that, the official talks between SEF and ARAT were soon restarted, accompanied by close people-to-people contacts in a speed, faster than ever before. 23 agreements were signed with China the counterpart during Ma's presidency. Among them, Economic Cooperation Framework Agreement (兩岸經濟合作架構協議), first part of it was signed in 2009, is both historic and the most important one which is expected to bring benefit to the bilateral trade that already totals USD 110 billion a year. [14] In addition, negotiations on weekend charted flights, direct shipping linkage and opening door to the tourists from China, etc. are soon reactivated and agreements on these issues are also quickly reached; at the same time, deregulation on Taiwan's investment -- especially 12-inch fab production facilities -- in China and China's investment in Taiwan began to speed up which haunted the opposition party and was questioned as a step for China to penetrate and weaken Taiwan.

Unintended Consequences

On November 17th, 2015, a centurial meeting was held in Singapore which President Ma from Taiwan and President Xi from China met and broke the record set in past 66 years that leaders of both side never met. As the *New York Times* reporter described the scene,[15]

> *Mr. Xi and Mr. Ma began their brief talks with a handshake that went on for more than a minute, with both men smiling broadly and turning side to side so the hundreds of reporters in the meeting room at the Shangri-La Hotel in Singapore could document the moment. The meeting is a high point in the tow leaders' efforts to bridge the divisions of civil war and decades of animosity.*

It goes without saying all the world's focus and attention were totally attracted by this event. In the author's view, there are at least three takeaways in this important event, they being:-

President Ma's strategies toward China get paid

President Ma has been arranging, or even requesting, to meet President Xi in the public occasion, like the Asia Pacific Economic Cooperation (APEC) summit held in Indonesia (2013) and Beijing (2014). However, he never made it. Until this year, in the fourth meeting between Heads of Cross-Strait competent Authorities held in Guangzhou (廣州), China, Xi finally agreed to meet Ma.[16] Xi of course has his considerations;

however, no matter what kind of consequences it turned out to be, Xi's presence at the meeting is absolutely a success that Ma proves his strategies does work.

Xi is betting big

Before this Xi-Ma meeting, China used to mull over 'Taiwan problem' in the pattern of 'Party-to-Party'. However, after DPP won a landslide victory in Taiwan's 2014 '9 in 1' election, President Ma, then-Chairman of KMT, was forced to step down and gave up his party position. Now Xi cast aside the 'Party-to-Party' formula and met Ma in Singapore means he might be taking risk and 'implicitly' recognized the existence of the 'Republic of China (ROC)'. To go further, the identities of these two leaders are very clear, one (Xi) is the President of People's Republic of China (PRC), the other is the President of ROC. This could be very dangerous to Xi, especially if KMT lose the 2016 election again. Not to mention some opponents within CCP might wait for the chance to attack Xi for betting big on this meeting.[17]

The future is still vague

Put this Xi-Ma meeting on the table, their meeting absolutely symbolizes the leaders of both sides are taking important steps toward peace. To nobody's surprise, President Ma is leaving next year, the Chairperson of DPP, Tsai Ing-wen, is very possible to be the next President of Taiwan. Following the change of Taiwan's situation, Xi-Ma meeting might means nothing for the future of Cross-Strait relations. In other words, even Xi shook hands with Ma for more than a minute, once Tsai steps up as President and rejects to be framed by any prerequisites, the 'bridge', if there is as President Ma mentioned in the TV interview after the event,[18] might just disappear in a second. The road ahead, for both sides of Taiwan Strait, might be bumpy.

The event of Xi-Ma meeting is of course historic. However, the two leaders might never know what consequences could be brought to. The President in Taiwan, with an approval rating of 21.9 percent, tries his best to incorporate Xi to set up the limit for Taiwan might irritate the constituency which would use votes to express their resent as those happened in 1996 and 2000. DPP might have the highest support and be the ruling party in 2016. (Refer to Figure 1 & 2) On the other hand, KMT might lose its shirt at the track and be thrown into the ashes of history. The result will be a heavy blow to both 'bridge building' arrangement and 'united front' strategy.

As for Beijing, it could have been unaffected if it kept silent about the meeting. But Beijing never wants to be silent, as Bonnie Glaser has predicted, China might react harshly, including by taking punitive economic measures, suspending communication and cooperation mechanisms, stealing away some of Taiwan's diplomatic allies, or even using military coercion or force.[19] If these come true, Beijing will have to pay for not only losing the opportunity to persuade DPP be more cooperative on Cross-Strait issues, but also losing the legal basis to claim the sovereignty over the South China Sea, if DPP counters China by cooperating with the US on the same issue. All these will be the unintended consequences that President Ma and President Xi won't look for but are possible to be a reality.

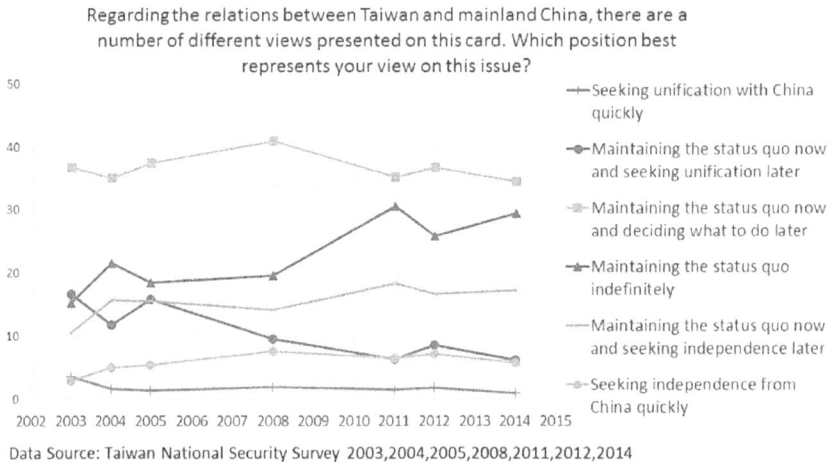

Regarding the relations between Taiwan and mainland China, there are a number of different views presented on this card. Which position best represents your view on this issue?

— Seeking unification with China quickly

— Maintaining the status quo now and seeking unification later

— Maintaining the status quo now and deciding what to do later

— Maintaining the status quo indefinitely

— Maintaining the status quo now and seeking independence later

— Seeking independence from China quickly

Data Source: Taiwan National Security Survey 2003,2004,2005,2008,2011,2012,2014

Figure 1. Taiwanese View Toward Cross-Strait Relations[20]

Taiwanese People's Conditionality of Preference
on relations with mainland China, 2003-2014

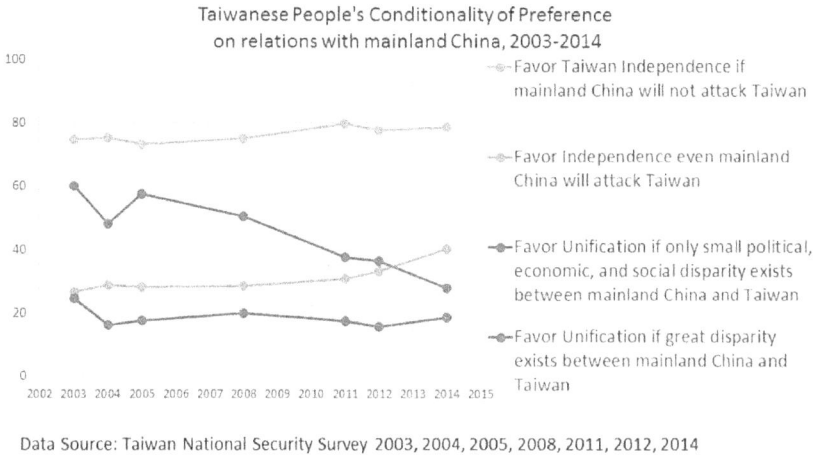

Data Source: Taiwan National Security Survey 2003, 2004, 2005, 2008, 2011, 2012, 2014

Figure 2. Taiwanese People's Conditionality of Preference on Relations with Mainland China, 2003-2014[21]

The Implications for East Asia

To sum up, there won't be a single answer to the question on what cross-strait relations might bring to East Asia. Frankly speaking, the answer depends on who is asking the question.

In general, the region East Asia, composed by at least 8 political entities (including Hong Kong and Macau), is still a powerhouse to the world's economy. Quite a bit of countries around the world, or even Taiwan itself, rely on trade with China so much. So if we want to discuss Cross-Strait relations with all the terms that economists and financial professionals used to use, the answer will be positively like 'closer contacts led by Taiwan's and China's government will absolutely bring peace and prosperity to the region'. Not to mention, the countries in this region are something like members incorporated in the same production line. In that sense, 'peace and prosperity' will be the most possible result that a closer Cross-Strait relationship will lead to.

Even in term of international politics, there's great hope. The Taiwan Strait has been pointed out as one of the 'hot spots' for possible conflicts in Asia.[22] If these two governments could gather and meet in regular pattern, as Ma touts 'institutionalized', they can communicate and try their best to avoid misperception. That hostility since 1949 might have the chance to disappear, and in turn lower the possibility to conflict.

However, there's also risk there. From a geopolitical view, the biggest risk is the Great Powers' misperception and the change of their attitude. As mentioned before, President Ma's grand strategy is to 'rapprochement with China, ally with the US and be friend with Japan'. If Taiwan and China getting closer and closer, or Taiwan further echoes China's claim on 'One China', 'sovereignty over the South China Sea', etc., that means Taiwan is absolutely unable to make use of the same-distance diplomacy and bound to 'Finlandize'. If that's the case in East Asia, then the US and its strong allies like Japan will possibly reconsider their cooperation with Taiwan.

Besides, US is now aggressively pursuing a strategy which can show its will and also redistribute its resources toward Asia, labeled as 'Pivot to Asia (or 'Rebalance Towards Asia'), the only possible target is 'China'. However, the US is still trapped by some other international or domestic issues that will force it to find new allies (e.g. Vietnam, India) or reconsolidate its relations with traditional allies (e.g. South Korea, Japan) in Asia. If Taiwan is excluded from those allies, we can forecast the US and Japan, and the others involved might directly deal with China without taking Taiwan's position into account.[23] At the same time, there will be more and more scholars and practitioners in the world who will promote 'giving up Taiwan, securing US's interests' theory,[24] let Taiwan's voice be diminished and Taiwan's interests damaged. Once the US, as well as China, becomes assertive in dealing with the South China Sea issues, East Asia might be locked in a very dangerous situation.

From China's view, the scene is different from that of the US's view. Compared with President Chen Shui-bian, President Ma apparently gives great hopes to Xi's China on 'unification'. China might feel the wrong way and have a adverse impression that it can unite with Taiwan in a couple of years. Now the election in 2016 seems to contradict China's wishes, China might give up thoughts on 'peaceful unification' and bluntly use force. Thought many observers of cross-strait relations affirm that China needs peaceful environment to develop it economy and will not be possible to use force against Taiwan, however, my personal observation, on the contrary, is that China will be reasonable enough to deal with all kinds of problems but not including 'Taiwan problem.' In a nutshell, shadow of war follows when the wrong hopes are shattered.

There are no absolute answers to any specific questions. For the time being, development of cross-strait relations seems to bring more risks than opportunities to East Asia. The US, Japan, and other democratic allies should not just hail on the historic moment of cross-strait relations , but have to give more concrete support – close trade, cultural exchange, even arms sales, etc. – to Taiwan and help diversify its interests to the other areas.[25] On the other hands, China's ambition to claim sovereignty over the South China Sea should be continually challenged and counter-balanced, if it's not like that, then the future of Taiwan is doomed. An aggressive China will not just take Taiwan, but also bring great dangers to Asia as a whole.

Endnotes

1   Yuan-kang Wang, 'Taiwan Public Opinion on Cross-Strait Security Issues,' **Strategic Studies Quarterly**, Vol. 7, Issue 2 (Summer/2013), p. 93.

2   'China, Taiwan and a Meeting After 66 Years,' **The New York Times**, Nov. 3, 2015. http://www.nytimes.com/2015/11/04/world/asia/leaders-of-china-and-taiwan-to-meet-for-first-time-since-1949.html?_r=0 (Accessed: Nov. 4, 2015)

3   During this period, Beijing called Taipei with the term, 'Chiang Gangsters' (蔣幫); and Taipei, vice versa, responded with 'Communist Bandits'(共匪).

4   Matthew Quest, 'The Lessons of the Bandung Conference,' **Spunk Library** (website), unknown date. http://www.spunk.org/texts/pubs/lr/sp001716/bandung.html

5   Yan Anlin, 'Cross-Taiwan Straits Relations and Beijing's Taiwan Policy Adjustment Since 1979,' in Kevin G. Cai, ed. **Cross-Taiwan Straits Relations Since 1979: Policy Adjustment and Institutional Change Across the Straits** (Canada: University of Waterloo, 2011), p. 22. 'Three Links' refer to 'air, shipping and postal services across the Straits'; 'Four Exchanges' refer to 'academic, cultural, sports, science and technological exchanges'.

6   'Three Nos' means 'No contact, No Negotiation, No Compromise'. Chiang Ching-Kuo's policy toward China was also interpreted as 'Separate Taiwan From China' (獨台).

7   SEF subordinates to the official department established in the same year, Mainland Affairs Council (Mac), Executive Yuan.

8   Then-Chairman of the Mainland Affairs Council, Su Chi, defined the basis as '1992 Consensus' for the 1993 talk in 2000. The content of this consensus is 'One China, Respective Interpretations' (一中各表).

9   'Four Noes One without' is Chen Shui-bian's political pledge which means he will not,

    1.   Declare independence of Taiwan;

    2.   Change the national title;

    3.   Include the doctrine of 'special state-to-state relations' in the Constitution;

4. Promote a referendum on unification or independence; and the last,

5. Without abolishing the National Unification Council, only if China promised not to use military force against Taiwan.

Refer to 'President Chen's 520 Inaugural Speech: Taiwan Stands Up: Advancing to an Uplifting Era (Excerpt),' Mainland Affairs Council, May 20th, 2000. http://www.mac.gov.tw/english/ english/macpolicy/cb0520e.htm,

10   'The New Year Message from the President: Originally One China Does Not Matter According to the Constitution', **United Daily**, January 1, 2001.

11   According to Hsiao-Chi Hsu, Chen's move is more like a manipulation of domestic politics, not to Mention DPP is suffered seriously in the 2005 election. Hsiao-chi Hsu, 'Domestic Vulner- ability and Nationalist Propaganda: Taiwan's National Unification Council Campaign in 2006,' **Issues and Studies**, Vol. 46, No. 4 (Dec. 2010); pp. 37-72.

12   'Su chi: Constructing the scheme of 'Rapprochement with China, Ally with the US, Be Friend with Japan,' **Herald Today**, Dec. 24, 2009. http://www.herald-today.com/content.php?sn=1090 (〈蘇起：建構「和中、友日、親美」格局〉，今日報導，2009年12月24日。) Though he apparently prioritized the relationship among Taiwan-and-China, Taiwan-and-US and Taiwan-and-Japan. He contradictorily insisted that these bilateral relations should be parallel and equal.

13   However, the government seems never tell the people if it did reach an agreement with China which will guarantee China's promise to truce and the feasibility of Taiwan's 'Viable Diplomacy'.

14   'Historic Taiwan-China Trade Deal Takes Effect,' **BBC News**, Sep. 20, 2010. http://www.bbc.com/news/world-asia-pacific-11275274

15   'Leaders of China and Taiwan Talk for Peace Across the Strait,' **The New York Times**, Nov. 7, 2015. http://www.nytimes.com/2015/11/08/world/asia/presidents-china-taiwan-meet-shake-hands-singapore.html?_r=0

16   According to the former Vice Chairman of the Mainland Affairs Council, Chong-pin Lin, the main reasons that motivate Xi to meet Ma are:

1. China is more and more assertive in the South China Sea and hence more possible to conflict with the US, and some other ASEAN members. Based

on that, China needs to incorporate Taiwan into a 'United Front' and make sure Taiwan will not accept the United Nations Convention on Law of the Sea (UNCLOS) and give up the 'Nine-dash-line' sovereign claims.

2. Beijing is not comfortable with DPP's coming victory in 2016 election. Xi worried that DPP might not be easy to control. The best option is to set up a frame with President Ma on the future of Taiwan and the direction of cross-strait relations.

Refer to 'Chong-pin Lin on Xi-Ma Meeting: A Concept of "One Country Two Government",' **United Daily**, Nov. 4, 2015. http://udn.com/news/story/1/1294018-林中斌評馬習會：「一國兩府」概念成真 (〈林中斌評馬習會：「一國兩府」概念成真〉聯合報，2015年11月4日。)

17 'Out of "KMT-CCP" framework, Ma-Xi Meeting Sends "ROC" into the Big Gamble,' **The Initium Media**, Nov. 8, 2015. https://theinitium.com/article/20151108-taiwan-Xi-and-Ma-summit-ROC-Issue/ (〈脫離國共框架馬習會把「中華民國」送入豪賭〉，端傳媒，2015年11月8日。)

18 'Ma Built a Bridge in Ma-Xi meeting Ma: Make Sure the Successor Follows the Traffic Rules,' **Storm Media**, Nov. 11, 2015. http://www.storm.mg/article/73655 (〈馬習會為繼任者搭橋馬：先確定能遵守交通規則〉風傳媒，2015年11月11日。)

19 Bonnie S. Glaser and Jacqueline Vitello, 'Xi Jinping's Great Game: Are China and Taiwan Headed Towards Trouble?' **National Interest** (website), Jul. 16, 2015. http://nationalinterest.org/feature/xi-jinpings-great-game-are-china-taiwan-headed-towards-13346

20 Source: 'Taiwan and Mainland China in Talks? Here are the 5 Things You Need to Know About What Taiwanese People are Thinking.' **The Washington Post**, Nov. 6, 2016. https://www.washingtonpost.com/news/monkey-cage/wp/2015/11/06/taiwan-and-mainland-china-in-talks-here-are-the-5-things-you-need-to-know-about-what-taiwanese-people-are-thinking/

21 Source: 'Taiwan and Mainland China in Talks? Here are the 5 Things You Need to Know About What Taiwanese People are Thinking.' **The Washington Post**, Nov. 6, 2016. https://www.washingtonpost.com/news/monkey-cage/wp/2015/11/06/taiwan-and-mainland-china-in-talks-here-are-the-5-things-you-need-to-know-about-what-taiwanese-people-are-thinking/

22   UkHeo and Shale A. Horowitz, **Conflict in Asia: Korea, China-Taiwan, and India-Pakistan** (Westport, Conn.: Greenwood Publishing Group, 2003), pp. 25-66.

23   For example, US sent a warship to the South China Sea and challenges China's territorial claims in the contested waters. 'Navy Destroyer Sails Near Disputed Chinese Islands,' **USA Today**, Oct. 30, 2015. http://www.usatoday.com/story/ news/world/2015/10/26/navy- china-south-china-sea/ 74652962/

24   Bill Owens, "America Must Start Treating China as a Friend," **Financial Times**, November 17, 2009. http://www.ft.com/intl/cms/s/0/69241506-d3b2-11de-8caf-00144feabdc0.html#axzz1RXebUtOH; Bruce Gilley, 'Not So Dire Straits: How the Finlandization of Taiwan Benefits U.S. Security, ' **Foreign Affairs,** Vol. 89, No. 1 (January/February 2010), pp. 44-60. http://www. foreignaffairs.com/ articles/65901/bruce-gilley/not-so-dire-straits

25   DPP's Presidential candidate, TsiaIng-wen, proposed a 'New Southward Policy' at a banquet to mark the 29th anniversary of the DPP's founding on Sep. 22, 2015.The policy seems to redirect Taiwan's focus on Southeast and South Asia. 'DPP's Tsai Ing-wen Proposes New "Southward Policy",'**Formosa News**, Sep. 22, 2015.http://englishnews.ftv.com.tw/Read.aspx?sno=787D3BFE219CB628 78FF904E0161EBBD

PART - IV

Measures for Forging Indo-Pacific Security Cooperation

Who are who in the realm of Western Pacific regional in/security?

Dr Victor Sumsky

Three Types of Regional Security Structures

Structures for regional cooperation in the field of security that exist today in the Western Pacific are represented by

- A sum of US-led bilateral military alliances, evolving lately into a "Power Web" in which junior partners are also developing ties between themselves (naturally, with Washington's endorsement);

- A set of multilateral dialogue platforms (namely, ASEAN Regional Forum, East Asian Summit and ADMM+) built on the principle of ASEAN centrality but still formally unconnected;

- Shanghai Cooperation Organization (SCO), in which its founders China, Russia and four Central Asian states are now joined by India and Pakistan, with Iran widely perceived as the next full-time member.

Historical Backgrounds

The Cold War origins of bilateral military alliances between the US and such countries as Japan, South Korea, Australia, New Zealand, Thailand and the Philippines need no special proof. Born in the mid-20th century, they were designed to contain America's Communist adversaries – the Soviet Union and Red China. More than fifty years later they still serve the basic need of safeguarding American regional and global dominance against the same potential competitors (notwithstanding all the differences between the China of Chairman Mao and that of President Xi on the one hand, as well as the Soviet Union and the Russian Federation on the other hand).

As the first of the ASEAN-centered dialogue platforms, ARF was conceived in that brief post-Cold War moment when great power rivalry looked like a matter of the past and ever-growing economic interdependence was considered the greatest guarantee of regional stability and peace. Dynamic East Asia was anticipating an age of evolutionary development and prosperity, and the proverbial ASEAN way (that is, reliance on gradualism, the spirit of compromise and win-win principles) was adopted to address a variety of non-traditional challenges. More or less the same philosophy underpinned the formation of EAS and ADMM+.

Prior to the creation of the Shanghai Five in 1996 (which evolved into SCO five years later) its future members were primarily concerned with creating secure neighbourhoods for each other through solution of unresolved territorial issues, demilitarization of borders and a formal subscription to a set of confidence building measures (including detailed agreements on how to restore confidence if and when it is shattered). Apart from that, since the early post-Soviet days the SCO founders saw religious extremism as a major threat to their domestic stability and development. A commonly held view that favorable regional environment was essential for national modernization efforts had very much to do with the emergence of SCO and remains its fundamental feature.

The Issue of 'Effectiveness and Shortcomings'

No attempt to identify the relative strengths and weaknesses of the security structures mentioned above will lead to sound conclusions unless these structures are evaluated against the background of quickly changing historical and strategic realities. Most importantly, the movement towards a polycentric world that was proceeding in an evolutionary way throughout the two post-Cold War decades, has lately acquired a different mode and a different tempo – less 'sanguine' and more 'choleric', more error-, accident- and conflict-prone. With the rise of such contradictions between major powers this may eventually defy win-win solutions. While this is not to say that grave troubles are imminent, no one can be sure that existing security structures are capable of contributing together to a larger Indo-Pacific (or pan-Asian) security mechanism.

The US-led Alliances

Collectively, the US-led bilateral alliances possess a formidable fighting potential which is permanently tested during joint military exercises. They have an obvious, strong leader who is skillfully exploiting its partners' uneasy feelings about the economic and political rise of China. Since the idea of containing the latter has a degree of support among the military and political elites of some Asian nations – both traditional US allies and newly emerging partners, it is quite probable that the "Power Web" contemplated by American strategists will continue to grow. However, this trend is unlikely to result in a pan-Asian security system. At the time when transition towards polycentrism in regional and global affairs is gaining momentum along with attempts to undermine such a process, neither China, nor Russia will join this American project (not to speak of the fact that American maneuvers evoke mixed reactions even among the US allies). In short, this is a road towards Indo-Pacific Insecurity – a new era of confrontation and polarization of forces.

ASEAN-centric Dialogue Platforms

Inclusiveness is an obvious strong point of ASEAN-centric security structures. In terms of membership, a dialogue platform such as ARF fully deserves the name of an Indo-Pacific forum. But in the midst of strategic distrust that is growing all across the Western Pacific the ASEAN-centric bodies start to look somewhat less relevant than even 3 or 4 years ago. The sharpening of US-China contradictions contributes to centripetal tendencies in ASEAN. Eventually this threatens either to diminish the role of the platforms where ASEAN's function is that of a 'cornerstone', or to create a situation in which this role will de facto pass to someone else. The informality of ASEAN's internal procedures as well as lack of coordination between ARF, EAS and ADMM+ does not help either. Although in many ways ASEAN is a tested and worthy candidate for a position of importance in the future polycentric world, its habitual political style hardly correlates with the turbulent world of today.

Shanghai Cooperation Organization

While relations between China and Russia as the pillars of SCO are already close enough, America's simultaneous attempts to cut Europe away from Russia and to drive a wedge between Asia and China stimulate Moscow and Beijing to explore new avenues of cooperation. In 2014-15 the two powers have begun to jointly work on what may become a megaproject to integrate Eurasia in infrastructural, energy, financial and economic terms. Remarkably, this is also the time when – after years of weighing and deliberation – a decision to bring in India and Pakistan is finally taken, and solution of the 'Iranian problem' is making it possible to proceed still further down the road of the SCO expansion. Chaos in the Middle East and the emergence of ISIL keep the SCO members highly alerted to transnational terrorist threats, and interactions between their military and intelligence bodies are becoming more motivated and more systematic. Thus, SCO is turning into an organization of a truly Indo-Pacific scale, with a combined economic, diplomatic and military potential that allows it to support polycentrism in international affairs not just verbally. No one would claim, of course, that all contradictions between the SCO members (which have never been a secret) are about to be resolved. Nevertheless, at this point a trend towards mutual understanding and cooperation is clearly prevailing over a trend in the opposite direction.

Concluding Remarks and Questions

The present level of tensions in the Western Pacific is a reflection of intensifying competition between the 'forces of hegemony' and the 'forces of polycentrism'. Does this situation preclude the formation of a Pan-Asian security structure or is it still possible?

Of the three types of security structures in the Western Pacific, those related to ASEAN and SCO look like having sufficient mutual compatibility for a dialogue on Pan-Asian security cooperation. But is there enough political will on both sides to move along this way?

If the answer is no, it will definitely not help in terms of building a polycentric world. However, even in this case the process will not stop altogether – especially if China and Russia continue to cooperate at least like they do today.

If the answer is yes, one may be sure that the US (along with its staunchest allies) will not accept it humbly and quietly. Therefore, intensified political struggle may accompany both the emergence of the polycentric world and the formation of a pan-Asian security structure. In this scenario, tensions in the Western Pacific are likely to rise to a still higher level before they are eased.

Indian Ocean Security Cooperation

Commodore Lalit Kapur (Retd)

The Paris terror attacks of 13 November 2015 have once again brought home to that the world is a far from safe place, particularly when dealing with the non-traditional threats to security. The lesson is not new – we have the example of New York and 9/11, Bali in 2002, Madrid in 2004, London in 2005, Mumbai in 2006 and 2008, Norway in 2011, the Boston marathon in 2013, the Charlie Hebdo attacks earlier this year, the downing of Metrojet 9268 on 31 October, the Beirut bombing of 11 November, and so many others one can think of. What this shows us is that the world is not a safe place.

If land spaces even in advanced countries with well-developed governance systems are insecure, the insecurities at sea, which belongs to no country and has no meaningful governance mechanism to talk of, are far greater. The seas are essentially ungoverned territory, where the writ of no state is applicable. Globalisation and the vastly increased need of the oceans for transportation has led to the emergence numerous non-traditional threats in this ungoverned or poorly governed space, including piracy, maritime terrorism, traffic in narcotics, arms and people, environmental pollution, illegal fishing and illegal migration. Talk of murder for sport, bonded labour, slavery, renegade ships, unregulated floating armouries etc. has not really percolated into the public discourse, but all this does happen at sea. An idea of the nature of the environment comes from a video clip embedded in a New York Times report of 20 July 2015[1], which will be screened for you now.

Who is to assume responsibility for security in the IOR, given the cocktail of nationalities found on ships? Security for what—Is it for territory, property, citizens or interests? Till the Second World War, it was provided by Great Britain. The colonial age has, however, passed. Indian Ocean littorals are independent and will strongly resent any attempt by external powers to govern the sea spaces, even if these powers had some interest in doing so. But the fact is that the variety of non-traditional threats does not impact on external powers except indirectly; for them, accepting the losses involved due to the absence of a security mechanism is far cheaper than providing for it. The impact is felt most by the people and trade of the region, which is why it is important that a regional initiative emerges to tackle this problem.

The need for a regional security mechanism is thus self-evident. But what type of security are we talking about? Is it of territory, interests, property or the life of citizens? The world, and particularly the IOR, has become conditioned to thinking of security in traditional, zero-sum, territorial terms. Getting the widely disparate nations of the IOR to unite to tackle traditional threats will remain a chimera, at least for the foreseeable future.

But there is one area where the interests of all IOR littorals converge – that is in ensuring free movement of trade. This is a common interest for all littorals, irrespective of their race, colour or religion. Now traditional challenges to free movement of trade that come with national conflict will remain, but a regional security mechanism that seeks to counter such challenges will have to step on the toes of the UN Security Council as well as the countries directly affected, which include extra-regional powers with global interests. In my opinion, such an organisation is a non-starter, at least for now. The wide varieties of non-traditional challenges to maritime security that have exploded into public discourse during the recent years, some created by nature and others by man, however, offer a ripe focal area for regional security mechanisms. The need, particularly to tackle challenges created by man, is to create effective regional governance mechanisms that nullify the immense advantages obtained by both organised and un-organised criminals due to the trans-national, ungoverned nature of the maritime environment.

The structure, objectives and operating principles of such an organisation is the subject of another paper being presented at this seminar, but I will venture to say that it has to be consensus based. It will be necessary to carry all nations of the region as well as all extra-regional stakeholders along; governance (and security) without this consensus is not going to be feasible. Instead of creating a new mechanism, the more productive approach would be for an existing organisation to take up the responsibility.

Cooperative mechanisms in the IOR are few. Mechanisms with pan-regional vision and a security role include the Indian Ocean Rim Association, the Indian Ocean Naval Symposium and the Indian Navy's Exercise EX MILAN. There are a host of sub-regional organisations, including SAARC, GCC, Southern African Development Community (SADC), the Indian Ocean Commission and the Indian Ocean Tuna Commission (IOTC). Then there are piracy specific organisations like ReCAAP, CGPS, CTF 151, the EU Naval Force Somalia (otherwise known as Operation Atlanta) and multi-national maritime security missions such as CTF 150 (for the Red Sea, Gulf of Aden, Gulf of Oman and Indian Ocean) and CTF 152, for the Persian Gulf. Finally, there are bilateral, tri-lateral and in some cases multilateral structures, mostly in a nascent stage at present, intended more for confidence building than providing any real security. Examples are the Coordinated Patrols India does with Indonesia and Thailand, its trilateral with Sri Lanka and Maldives, budding security arrangements with Mauritius and Seychelles, the Eyes in the Sky and MSSI etc.

The India Ocean Rim Association is widely seen as the mechanism most likely to take on the security cooperation mantle. It has 21 members (Australia, Bangladesh, Comoros, India, Indonesia, Iran, Kenya, Madagascar, Malaysia, Mauritius, Oman, Seychelles, Singapore, South Africa, Sri Lanka, Tanzania, Thailand, UAE, Yemen and Somalia, whose membership was approved in 2014 and is currently being processed). It has seven dialogue partners: China, Egypt, France, Germany, Japan, UK and USA and two observers: the Indian Ocean Tourism Organisation (IOTO) and the Indian Ocean Research Group (IORG). While the membership is no doubt a cause for satisfaction, the absence of 17

Indian Ocean littorals (Bahrain, Djibouti, Egypt, Eritrea, Iraq, Israel, Jordan, Kuwait, Maldives, Mozambique, Myanmar, Pakistan, Qatar, Reunion, Saudi Arabia, Sudan and Timor Leste) is a handicap for any consensus-based security mechanism. Extra-regional powers without a voice, even as dialogue partner in IORA, include the EU, Russia, South Korea and Taiwan.

It is worth looking at the stated objectives of the IORA. These include:-

- To promote the sustained growth and balanced development of the region and of member states, and to create common ground for regional economic cooperation.

- To focus on those areas of economic cooperation which provide maximum opportunities to develop shared interests and reap mutual benefits. Towards this end, to formulate and implement projects for economic cooperation relating to trade facilitation and liberalisation, promotion of foreign investment, scientific and technological exchanges, tourism, movement of natural persons and service providers on a non-discriminatory basis, and the development of infrastructure and human resources inter alia poverty alleviation, promotion of maritime transport and related matters, cooperation in the fields of fisheries trade, research and management, aquaculture, education and training, IT, health, protection of the environment, agriculture, disaster management

- To explore all possibilities and avenues for trade liberalisation, to remove impediments to, and lower barriers towards, free movement of goods services, investment and technology within the region.

- To encourage close interaction of trade and industry, academic institutions, scholars and the people of the Member States without any discrimination among Member States and without prejudice to obligations under other regional economic and trade cooperation arrangements.

- To strengthen cooperation and dialogue among member states in international flora on global economic issues, and where desirable to develop shared strategies and take common positions in the international fora on issues of mutual interest and

- To promote cooperation in development of human resources, particularly through closer linkages among training institutions, universities and other specialised institutions of the Member States.

The salient principles of IORA's functioning are as follows:-

- Respect for sovereign equality, territorial integrity, political independence, non-interference in internal affairs, peaceful coexistence and mutual benefit.

- Membership is open to all IO Rim states who subscribe to objectives and principles and are willing to undertake commitments under charter.

- All decisions are by consensus.

- Bilaterals and issues likely to generate controversy and be an impediment to regional cooperation are to be excluded from deliberations.

- Cooperation is without prejudice to rights and obligations of member states under other cooperation arrangements, which will not apply to all IORA members.

- Member driven approach to attain goals and objectives.

- Promotion of principles of good governance to enable smooth implementation of programmes

A look at IORA's institutional mechanisms. The following are relevant:-

- Apex level is Council of (Foreign) Ministers (COM).

- COM elects Chair and Vice Chair of IORA for two year period. The current chair is Indonesia, vice-chair is South Africa.

- The next level is Committee of Senior Officials (CSO) appointed by member states. It reviews implementation of decisions taken by COM, establishes priorities for economic cooperation; develops, monitors and coordinates work programmes and mobilises resources for financing programmes. CSO submits periodic reports to COM and refers policy matters for their decision.

- Subsidiary bodies are Indian Ocean Rim Business Forum (IORBF), Indian Ocean Rim Academic Group (IORAG) and Working Group on Trade and Investment (WGTI).

- A troika comprising chair, vice-chair and previous chair reviews progress, establishment of additional mechanisms, policy direction to IORA institutions and appointment of Secretary General.

- Working Group of Heads of Mission (WGHM) in Pretoria reviews work programme presented by Chair and acts as a follow up mechanism.

- Secretariat headed by Secretary General based at Ebene, Mauritius monitors implementation of policy decisions and work programmes presented by COM. Current Secretary General is KV Bhagirath.

- IORA is financed by contributions from member states, based on criteria decided by COM.

Let us look at the security related declarations by IORA. These are as follows:-

- The Bangalore Communiqué of Nov 2011 identified six priority areas for cooperation, including maritime security and piracy, disaster risk reduction and fisheries management.

- The Gurgaon Communiqué of Nov 2012 identified piracy as a serious concern threatening maritime commerce; recognised that weak governance and instability in parts of the IOR contributed to rise in transnational organised crime; welcomed emphasis on maritime security cooperation and reaffirmed importance of maintaining freedom of navigation and safety and security of SLOCs. It also underscored importance of better preparedness to fight natural and other disasters in maritime domain, identified cooperation in SAR and training in Oil Spill Response as relevant areas for IORA, acknowledged need to develop cooperation to evolve disaster management strategies and operational processes.

- The Perth Communiqué of Nov 2013 adopted the name IORA in lieu of IORARC; identified IORA as lead body in promoting regional collaboration across the IO Rim; expressed a desire to broaden and deepen efforts in IORA to bolster maritime safety and security; sought concrete options to enhance counter-piracy cooperation, including through improved maritime information-sharing and stronger legal capacity and laws; and recognised that all IORA members had a stake as invited participants in IONS, considered it important that IORA work in maritime safety and security and disaster management align with and complement IONS initiatives in these areas

- The Perth Communiqué of Oct 2014 committed IORA to work closely with IONS and relevant organisations to address shared maritime and security challenges that threaten SLOCs and transportation in the IO, notably piracy and terrorism.

- The IORA Maritime Cooperation Declaration Padang Oct 2015 resolved to address maritime challenges such as illegal, unreported and unregulated fishing, piracy, irregular movements of people, marine pollution, drugs trafficking, illegal trafficking in wild life, disasters and climate change by:-

  - Enhancing coordination & communication between and among national maritime agencies and authorities and other relevant fora.

- Promoting region's capacity for disaster risk management and SAR.

- Enhancing cooperation on maritime safety, security and environment protection.

From the foregoing, it comes out that the IORA has a limitation in that 16 of the IOR littorals are not members, it is not a treaty level body (like NATO or Warsaw Pact) and its charter is not enforceable; the charter does not contain any security related objectives; the apex level is the Council of Foreign Ministers who have no security responsibility; and there is no subsidiary body for security. Consequently, the general impression of the IORA is "much talk, little action", at least on the security front. There is pressing need for a linked security construct. Indonesia's initiative towards an IORA Concord for adoption at an IORA Summit in March 2017 supported by IORA, may see evolution beyond talk.

The next mechanism is the Indian Ocean Naval Symposium (IONS). Its membership is better than IORA in that Maldives, Mozambique, Myanmar, Pakistan, Saudi Arabia, Timor Leste and UK are members. On the other hand, from the IORA member list, Comoros and Kenya are not, while Madagascar and Malaysia are observers, along with China and Japan. The key objectives of IONS are:-

- To promote a shared understanding of the maritime issues facing littoral nation states of the Indian Ocean and the formulation of a common set of strategies designed to enhance maritime security.

- To strengthen the capability of all nation states of the Indian Ocean to address present and anticipated challenges to maritime security and stability.

- To establish and promote a variety of trans-national, maritime, cooperative mechanisms designed to mitigate maritime security concerns within the Indian Ocean.

- To develop interoperability in terms of doctrines, procedures, organisation and logistic systems and operational processes so as to promote the development of regional naval capacities for speedy, responsive and effective HADR throughout the Indian Ocean Region.

IONS has two basic limitations, as follows:-

- It is limited to Navy level cooperation. It can address military and naval doctrine, naval procedures and training and technological compatibility, but cannot take on risk assessments, national security policy, rules of engagement, regional security regimes, agreements and arrangements.

- It must, therefore, be backed up by effective head of government, senior minister, senior official and academic level dialogue to deal with security, strategy and policy issues.

A word about Exercise MILAN, which commenced in 1995 and is held in Port Blair biennially.Australia, Bangladesh, Cambodia, India, Indonesia, Kenya, Malaysia, Maldives, Mauritius, Myanmar, New Zealand, Philippines, Seychelles, Singapore, Sri Lanka, Tanzania and Thailand participated in MILAN 2014. The exercise is a good initiative, but suffers from much the same infirmities as IONS and can at best help build tactical level cooperation.

The piracy specific mechanisms and the bilateral/trilateral can at best help build security at the sub-regional level, but cannot effectively address the Ocean as a whole. The following, thus emerge:-

- Maritime security is recognised as common interest for entire IOR. The Ocean faces both traditional and non-traditional challenges, but focus remains on traditional security.

- Non-traditional security issues stem from inadequate governance structures coupled with divided jurisdiction.

- All have trans-national linkages, cannot be addressed by individual nations.

- No dedicated global or regional governance mechanisms exist.

- Requirement is to prevent the use of maritime areas for illegal or anti-national activity and to secure movement of shipping.

Who is to address this requirement and take on responsibility? Should regional nations continue to bank on extra-regional powers or individual nations, or should they evolve a cooperative security mechanism? The fact is that regional nations seem currently content to supplement task forces set up by extra regional powers without assuming responsibility for a matter that has a deep impact on them. There is pressing need for regional security architecture to address non-traditional challenges to maritime security in the first instance. This architecture can address traditional issues once requisite levels of confidence and cooperation have been reached.

Objectives of Indo-Pacific Security Mechanism, Crystal Gazing on Structure, Governance and Funding Mechanism, Extra Regional Power Perspective

Dr Michael Pillsbury

I want to specially underline my gratitude before I attack USI. USI has gotten something of a free ride at this conference. There's a four page essay that's called a Concept Essay that's has been passed out to all of you and I want to object to it and focus my remarks on this four page essay. It's anonymous. There's no authors name so it could speak for all members of USI, which is something like 3000 retired officers, right? (15000 serving and retired officers, as corrected by the audience) 15000 serving and retired officers have managed to write an essay which insults equally China and the US. And I suppose we are expected to just ignore this Concept Essay in part because it is unsigned and in part because it pretends to be some sort of a description of current situation in the Indo-Pacific Region. Most of the briefings by Indian friends have been put up on the screen or talked about are very similar. Instead of saying America or China which are very common in United Nations or all over the world as the number one and number two economies of the world, instead of using America and China the term that has been used over and over again as 'extra territorial powers' and you also notice on the list of the Indian Ocean Association and Symposium, there are two powers missing each time the list is put up –America and China. Now there seems to be an assumption in the Concept Essay that's false that somehow China and America are so much at odds and have so much friction that we here in the Indian Ocean especially Indian brothers and sisters can organize the region, provide security to the entire Indian Ocean Region against China and America, because these two powers somehow don't get along. Well I wrote a book that says it's not true. The book is called "A Hundred Year Marathon" and like President Xi Zing Ping I say that there are elements of competition between the US and China which is unavoidable – mainly economic competition, competition to be number one in various ways and China has pulled ahead of us Americans in many ways in last ten years. The list is very long; one of the most striking things is the number of billionaires in America and China. It has nothing to do with nuclear weapons and stealth bombers but the number of billionaires in China now surpasses the number of billionaires in America. There are many indicators where China has pulled ahead of America. This is natural competition. The cooperation between US and China vastly outweighs the competition. The cooperation includes even to the point that recently our former Pacific commander at Montblair, proposed joint patrols of the Chinese Navy and the American Navy in the Indian Ocean to protect oil ships. Now all the lies and all the comments you have heard for two days and the USI Concept Essay by the anonymous person would be stunned at the idea of joint Chinese-American Navy Patrols but my book says that it is just the beginning of what has going on for last 40 years. In Chapter 12- secret projects between the US and China - one was to force the Yunnan to leave Cambodia, one was in Afghanistan, one was the weapons sales we made to China, pretty much according to their request to improve their torpedoes, artillery better jet fighters and receptors, quite a long list to strengthen the Chinese military. By some indicators our largest American Embassy in the world is in Beijing. The greatest number of assistance agreements in science and technology, environment you name it, is between the US and China. It goes by the shorthand term G-2- meaning global governance by two powers, coordinating their central bank interventions, meeting at the Bank of International Settlements (BIS) in Basel twice a year – the Federal Reserve Chairman and the Chinese Central Bank Chairman. So it's not many of our speakers but the Concept Essay that are simply blind to the deep cooperative between US-China who are number one and number two in the world, cooperating in all areas of the world, not excluding the IOR is somehow a place where we two "extra territorial powers" will not go.

Now there is one another thing where I have to really criticize the USI Concept Essay. China is actually helping India in a number of ways but America is helping Indian defence establishment enormously. If you go online and look at our structure there are foreign ministry people here, Mr. Chairman, foreign ministry people like to go to conferences, have security mechanisms but they can't commit troops, no foreign minister in the world has power to send troops, or ships to use force, it's done by the Heads of States. So there's a Defence Ministry at all capitals of the world. The defence ministry looks at capabilities of the Country. An Indian Admiral told me in 2001 that we don't really know what's going on in the Indian Ocean. Eventually the US sold P8 maritime surveillance aircrafts to give India the capability, to monitor what's going on deep into the Indian Ocean. Indian military officers brought up the need for C130J aircraft to quickly redeploy troops, including Special Forces along the northern border. American government approved the sale. Apache Helicopters that can fire hellfire missiles, it's a way to stop border intrusion and it has many other military uses and capabilities. India did not have anything close to it. The transaction was recently completed for the Apache helicopters to come to India, under Indian control. Part of all this sale of equipment, surveillance mechanisms, intelligence cooperation, defence trade and defence technology cooperation, all of this is chronicled every year in a meeting we call DPG and the Indian side and our side issue a joint statement every year to give the progress of the DPG – Defence Policy Group which just met two days ago in Washington. It alternates between Delhi and Washington. Each year I recommend to friends at USI that they read DPG Annual Statement. There are five groups under it and each group reports the military exchange programmes, the joint exercises, the participation in joint development of weapons, whether or not the US should help Indian with its new aircraft carrier designs. This is the real security mechanism in the IOR. If India had no capabilities in army, navy, airpower, cyber, space, and surveillance, India cannot provide security to the IOR. So I ask you- this USI anonymous author – who is helping India tremendously to improve its military and intelligence capabilities? The Americans. So why call us an 'extra territorial power"? Why insult the Americans? And if Chinese want to object it's their wish, but I'll object on their behalf, you shouldn't refer to China in this way. You are insulting the two great powers of this world while you expect no one to notice this kind of briefing and essay that some anonymous person should provide a security mechanism plan outside of the UN charter, outside the general norms of the international law especially tailored for the Indian Ocean and exclude China and America. Now that's covered a lot in the book where I describe the history of secret cooperation - I don't like the word secret between the US and China- the two militaries and two intelligent services. So as possible I should be softer on USI because perhaps you did not know the history of the 12 projects and more of the US-China secret cooperation. And because you did not know, you made a false assumption that US and China are somehow enemies who cannot cooperate in the Indian Ocean especially provoked by insults that we are extra territorial powers who have no role here. So the Eastern Commander is here himself and will be summing up the Valedictory Address of entire conference and I appeal to him to please include in his summing up my strong objections to the Concept Essay, to the framework, and to the idea that Indian Ocean belongs to India and the American strengthening of Indian Army, navy, air force and intelligent capability can just be ignored at an international scholarly conference. It would strike me if I was the valedictory speaker, I would take note of this objection and try maybe next year for USI's Concept Essay to be a bit more tactful about the power that has 15 trillion dollars GDP, that is my Country, the power that has close to it i.e. China, and be more modest about the power that recently just this year attained 2 trillion dollars GDP; it is a front page headline in your country " India reaches 2 trillion point", we reached this many decades ago, China reached it a long time ago, India should be more modest with 2 trillion dollars as an annual GDP and very weak armed forces, which my country has made a strategic decision to strengthen, but there is a limit to America's patience when they are increasingly insulted at international conferences. Thank you very much

An Indian Ocean Perspective on New Regional Security Mechanism — Objectives, Structure and Governance

Commander MH Rajesh

Introduction

The aim of this paper is to provide an Indian Ocean perspective on a new regional security mechanism- identifying its objectives, structure, and governance and funding. Since the countries in Indian Ocean Region (IOR) are not homogenous in economy, culture or strategic outlook, building a collective, consensual, pan ocean idea of security is a challenge in the region. Any future structure will have to base itself on some accepted global trends. Regional and pan ocean organisations already exist, however a pan ocean indigenous maritime security regime is yet to evolve in IOR. The ongoing anti-piracy campaign in the region highlights some lessons for future. That problem's origins and scope gives some pointers to the future if such a structure were to evolve. This paper examines the global trends for future, diversity, prospective structures, motivators and certain specific recommendations to improve maritime security in the region.

Defining the Indo Pacific

Rory Medcalf articulates that at the simplest level of understanding, the "Indo-Pacific" label means recognizing that the accelerating economic and security connections between the Western Pacific and the Indian Ocean, is creating a single strategic system[50]. It is a Maritime System of markets at one end and sources at other- balanced by Geopolitics.

If the line or ends get disturbed-world gets affected! A cursory glance at the Indo Pacific indicates that it is a very large construct which any single power will find hard to manage. So there has to be a manageable, 'Core Indo Pacific' where all the significant activities are taking place. This paper considers that the eastern limit of that core should be approximately 12000nm East of Africa. This is since the earth is round, navigationally, beyond half the earth's circumference subject to factors like canal sizes, ships have options to go the other way round; and therefore Indo Pacific becomes less relevant. There are some geographic disrupters of the idea too, such as opening up of Arctic's or a canal that China is planning in Nicaragua. If they fructify, the load of this line could change a little! Indo Pacific has certain distinct regional security complexes with diverse identities. Barry Buzan identifies them as South African Complex, the Horn of Africa Complex, Middle East Complex, South Asia Complex and East Asia Complex[51]. One of the key arguments of this paper is that since the region is too large security capacities will remain distributed within these complexes.

Pacific and IOR- Key Differences

If an Indian Ocean perspective is to be developed, differences between the IOR and Western Pacific is important to progress that aim. An Indian Ocean perspective to security structures could reflect this difference. Some key differences are stated below:-

Factor	Indian Ocean	Pacific
Diversity	High	Low
GDP	Low	High
Flash Points	Fragile States, Terror, Land	Evolved states, Territorial disputes, Sea
Climate Change Effect	High	Low
US presence	May wane	Resident power

Factor	Indian Ocean	Pacific
Structures	Multilateral Evolving	ASEAN based and Mini laterals
Maritime Security	Evolving (IORA/IONS)	Better (ADMM + EAMF, EAS), WPNS
Security Objectives	Liberal	Realist
Resources	Source of Oil	Consumer of Oil
Trade	Markets	Manufacturers
Demography	Young	Ageing

Table 1 Pacific and IOR- key differences

Global Trends Affecting Structures

The backdrop for a future Indian Ocean regional security mechanism will be set by certain salient predictions regarding the Indian Ocean. The dominant themes to consider are

- Rise of its Asian and African littorals at a historic pace[52]

- Future of power structure- Distributed over Centralised power structure?[53]

- Demography- The youth bulge, its impacts on productivity, migration and security[54]

- Race for resources- Interplay of scarcity of Energy, Food and Water[55].

- Climate Change and its impacts on Indian Ocean littorals[56]

Diversity- an Intrinsic Factor in IOR

The Indian Ocean littoral is home to thirty eight countries of myriad hues and a large number of equally diverse and relevant hinterland nations like Afghanistan. They are diverse in their race, culture, religions, economic structures, and strategic outlook with limited common ground to bind them together. The African littorals have clear demarcations with prosperous Southern Africa distinct from Eastern Africa. Horn of Africa has been a hot spot for many years and is being addressed by a separate security structure. Persian Gulf has a high value dynamic of its own. South Asia, South East Asia, Indian Ocean Islands and Australia are other separate sub regions. Fifty percent of prospective failed states are in the IOR littorals. In GDP terms, four out of top 20 (India, Indonesia, Australia, Saudi Arabia) and three out of bottom 20 (Comoros, Madagascar, Seychelles) are from Indian Ocean. Per capita GDP distribution is even more stark, with four out of top ten (Qatar, Singapore, Kuwait, and UAE) and three out of bottom 15 nations (Comoros, Madagascar, Mozambique) in the region. The average Qatari is 200 times richer than the average Malagasy[57]. There are five religions and several races in its shores. Yet at close to 9 tn US $ the region commands 11% of Global GDP which lends it a heft of its own[58]. This diversity and a lack of shared threat perception making creation of regional structures like that Europe's NATO difficult to envisage in IOR. Thinking through regional security mechanisms that complement the UN structures and statutes therefore, becomes a creative challenge.

Layers in the Security Structure

Search for objectives of a Regional Security Mechanism will lead to major security threats that were faced by Indian Ocean Region. For the purposes of this paper, a broader concept of security, beyond a military sphere has been adopted. Therefore this study of new regional security structure will essentially have two separate layers.

- First is a global **realist** layer, which will be linked to global events where any rising power will be balanced by other powers, either by internal security investments or by alliances. The new mental map of Indo-Pacific, US rebalance, One Belt One Road, TPP, RCEP are all linked to this economic and security balancing process[59]. Those structures will be exclusive in nature. The theme of this layer will be rise of China, future of US power and its relation to various other regional and middle powers.

- The second layer comprise a wider gamut of liberal, non-traditional domain of security for which there is a wider scope for participation along the Indian Ocean Region. This layer will deal with prevention of a non-traditional crisis and as first responders post crisis, under existing international law and UN statutes. This will be privileged to be an inclusive construct where external powers like China and US will be very much included.

Therefore, future IOR structures will have both traditional realist layers that focus on balance of power and the liberal inclusive structures that focus on non-traditional security. Both the layers will invariably influence each other. This is analogous to the events in the Pacific, where a liberal economic construct coexists with a realist, intensely rivalrous construct.

Objectives

The salient objectives of future Indian Ocean security architecture is explained as follows:-

- **Ensure Safe Maritime Commerce in IOR**. Most IOR nations belong to the undeveloped global south of the economic divide. These nations cannot achieve their true potential without maritime transport that enables 90% of global trade in volume. Therefore dividends of a stable maritime order could be a strong **common motivator** to bind the littorals. The unique feature of IOR is its nature as a maritime super conduit that connects the Atlantic and Pacific. Therefore, security of the IOR is of 'local' as well as **global** interest. That motivates extra regional powers to own a stake in security of IOR. Coalition operations against piracy in Western Indian Ocean are harbingers of that tendency. The major threat to maritime commerce could be a conventional confrontation in IOR, Piracy, and Terrorism. The structure must look at addressing these factors.

- **Aid in Ocean Resource Management**. One of the major security operations of the non-traditional realm in Indian Ocean has been current Anti-Piracy Operations. These operations have been going on for the past decade with billions spend by global powers. A closer look at piracy problem indicates that what lay at the heart of the Somali trouble was loss of fishing as a livelihood and dumping of toxic waste in Somali Coast by other nations[60]. Predictions indicate that food, energy and water are likely to be major resources that will be contested in the future[61]. One objective of the collective structure therefore should be to complement existing international structures that **arbitrate and motivate** order in the race for resources.

- **Develop Capacities to deal with Disasters/Environment/ Climate Change**. Climate Change raises sea levels, makes wet places wetter and dry, drier. Rise of sea levels Impact the IOR littorals directly. Global warming leads to depletion or relocation of fish stock, loss of arable land, and contamination of existing water resources forcing large scale migration[62]. Low lying Bangladesh and Maldives will be affected by rising sea levels. If oil catapulted Middle East to centre stage of Global Politics in last century, water shortage could be the theme of the future in dry Middle East. Though the rich and the poor nations will be affected, there is a distinct link between climate change vulnerability and GDP which makes the poorer countries more vulnerable to climate change[63]. Indian Ocean has some of the poorest countries in the world. Other than such a predicted change, unpredictable natural disasters such as earthquakes, tsunamis, floods and draughts are better managed collectively. Therefore an acceptable objective of the structure should be to **collectively deal** with the effects of disasters and climate change.

- **Prevent use of Oceans for Terrorism**. Indian Ocean has seen several serious terror incidents. In a recent incident, terrorists attempted to hijack a front line Pakistan Navy Frigate PNS Zulfiqar. The successful takeover could have resulted in catastrophic consequences to the entire region. In 2008, terror strikes in Mumbai were carried out by terrorists via sea from Karachi. The attacks on USS Cole and MV Limberg were carried out by terrorists at sea. There is a need to **address the threat of terrorism** through collective security structures. The sceptre of Al Qaeda has been active at sea, and ISIS could follow suit if unchecked. The Task Force 50 that operates in IOR has been formed with the aim of **'war on terror'**.

- **Management of Trans Ocean Crimes.** The opium producing regions of the world, namely the Golden Triangle, which involves Myanmar, Laos and Thailand and the Golden Crescent involving Iran, Pakistan and Afghanistan are on the Indian Ocean Rim. Drug trafficking has a close link to terrorism[64]. Trafficking of humans and small arms are other menace through the oceans which require collective redressal, since they are transnational crimes exploit the open oceans. **Cooperative management of Transocean crime** must an objective of these structures.

Existing Structures and its Contribution to Security

The major Countries/ Regional Organisations in IOR and currently has a security outlook that can continue to the future are as follows:-

- **Role of USA**. The present collective security framework exists under the UN umbrella and US pre-eminence. US has three unified command structures namely AFRICOM, CENTCOM and PACOM and three fleets Fifth, Sixth and Seventh fleets which focus on Indian Ocean littorals. Considering the recent creation of Africa Command and relevance of Middle East in the overall US strategy, Western Indian Ocean will continue to be of deep interest to the United States. With lesser reliance on Middle East oil, the interest in the region will slowly wane and shift to Africa. The rebalance to Asia has underlined that Western Pacific is a greater priority.

- **African Organisations**. The African Littorals have three organisations that are relevant to the IOR. Along the littorals, the regional organisation in the south half, the Southern African Development Council (SADC) has 15 members. It focuses on the prosperous Southern portion of Africa. In the North there is the Intergovernmental Agreement on Development (IGAD) which has 7 members. Both these organisations do not have a security element in their charter. However the most prominent African organisation, the African Union, has a Standing African Force. This is an evolving concept which has conducted its first military exercise in early Nov 15[65]. This is of interest to security in Africa, though it will be some time before a maritime element could emerge out of this regime. The appearance of a "security regime" in Africa is indeed inspiring.

- **Persian Gulf**. The littoral adjacent to Africa, the Gulf Cooperation Council (GCC) with 6 members is a significant organisation in IOR. It has a clear aspiration for security with a joint military force named the *Peninsular Shield Force* which has taken part in Iraq war and has also intervened in Bahrain during its uprising in 2011[66]. The GCC has the economic capacity to invest in a force and is one of the largest defence spenders ahead of Russia, France or rest of Middle East put together[67]. Due to deep ties in that region, US has been the principal provider of security to that region, with the Fifth Fleet located in Bahrain.

- **South Asia.** The most significant organisation in the sub region is South Asian association for Regional Cooperation (SAARC) with Bhutan, India, Maldives, Nepal, Pakistan, and Sri Lanka Afghanistan. This association promotes economics and socio-cultural development in the region. SAARC has an agreement on Rapid Response to Natural Disasters (ARRND), with an excellent disaster management knowledge portal[68]. They do not have a security regime or a standing force. However from the maritime perspective, the three littoral members, India, Srilanka and Maldives have NSA Level security dialogues on maritime security[69]. This is a separate structure from SAARC yet, of significance considering the strategic location of the three states astride the shipping lanes.

- **South East Asia**. There are two South East Asian organisations which can contribute to the *objectives* they are listed below:-

  ➢ Bay of Bengal Initiative (BIMSTEC). The Bay of Bengal Initiative for Multi-Sectoral Technical and Economic

Cooperation (BIMSTEC) involving Bangladesh, India, Myanmar, Sri Lanka, Thailand, Bhutan and Nepal. This has a separate working group focusing on Counter-Terrorism and Transnational Crime[70] and Environment and Natural Disaster Management- both led by India. BIMSTEC also has initiatives in place to deal with climate change led by Bangladesh.

➢ **ASEAN.**   At the Eastern Limits of IOR, constructs become ASEAN centric and gets truly Indo Pacific. ASEAN is the *literal and figurative fulcrum* of Indo Pacific Idea, to borrow the word fulcrum from President Jokowi who used it for Indonesia. The ASEAN derives its security perspective from the ADMM-Plus committee which has five IOR states, namely, Indonesia, Malaysia, Myanmar, Singapore, Thailand with two additional IOR states, Australia and India as Observers[71]. With China, Japan, Russian Federation, and the United States this body is structured right for security initiatives. ASEAN brings to IOR the South China Sea experience of maritime security and serving as a vital link between of the Indo Pacific. ASEAN nations have been beneficiaries of prosperity enabled by maritime commerce. That contributes to the cause of maritime security in IOR. The ASEAN experience also tells that organisations take a long time to evolve to develop a security regime. ADMM took shape 40 years after inception of ASEAN[72]. Compared to IOR structures, ASEAN has an evolved maritime outlook which has assisted formations of indigenous maritime cooperation between India Malaysia, Singapore and Indonesia to prevent piracy. Now that trend has to spread westwards. Again Medcalf[73] tells us that the 'gathering of leaders that founded the East Asia Summit on December 14, 2005 in Kuala Lumpur is the moment the contemporary Indo-Pacific was born'. Since ASEAN is the basic building block of structures in that region, Indo Pacific character is intrinsic there.

- **Ocean themed Groupings-IONS and IORA.** Indian Ocean also has two organisations that have an oceanic theme. They are the Indian Ocean Regional Association (IORA) and Indian Ocean Naval Symposium (IONS). Since the objective of the paper is consider organisations with potential for security structures in IOR a closer analysis was required of these two pan ocean structures:-

  - ➢ **IORA**. The rationale behind forming IORA was to unite littoral nations on the basis of the shared Indian Ocean identity for *socio-economic co-operation and other peaceful endeavours*[74]. The organisation was established in 1997 and has 20 members and six dialogue partners as on date, with three more lined up for membership. The fact that three members are lined up for membership shows its popularity. It has incrementally included maritime security in its agenda in the last five years. IORA is a 9 US $ Tn grouping, whereas its Pacific twin APEC is a 30tn US$, giant. As South Asia and Africa grows between 6-7% one has to be bullish on IORA. One should imagine IORA as a prospective 'APEC'.

  - ➢ **IONS**. IONS was established in 2008 to increase maritime co-operation among navies of Indian Ocean Region by providing an open and inclusive forum for discussion of regionally relevant maritime issues, develop common understanding for possible cooperative endeavours in future. IONS has 22 members and four observers[75]. IONS was inspired by the Western Pacific Naval Symposium, with which it shares 9 members.

  - ➢ **Comparisons-IOR, IONS and IORA**. The organisations are compared for exclusions and inclusions below:-

    - **Inclusiveness vis IOR**. Indian Ocean has 38 nations in its littorals including France and UK who possess Indian Ocean territories. While 22 nations are members in both IONS and IORA. That makes the IONS-IORA constructs fairly inclusive with 70% member ship of IOR littoral nations. China, US and Japan are observers or dialogue partners in both forums. Djibouti, Eritrea, Iraq, Sudan, Israel, Jordan, Qatar, Bahrain and Kuwait are members of neither IORA nor IONS presently.

- **What it Excludes**. Maldives, Myanmar, Pakistan, Saudi Arabia, Timur Leste are members of IONS but are not members of IORA. Maldives, Myanmar and Somalia are working towards IORA membership[76]. Whereas, Comoros, Kenya and Yemen are members of IORA and not IONS. Both *IONS and IORA do not have a total overlap in membership and roles.* Therefore IORA and IONS will have to coexist as two distinct organisations with overlapping roles for the time being.

➤ **IORA and Maritime Security**. A review of the evolution of IORA through a study of its communique indicates that IORA has incrementally included security in its ambit of concerns[77]. It is essentially a political group, whereas the natural organisation to response to crisis is the nearest Coast Guards or Navies of the region represented collectively through IONS. Meaningful maritime security requires a closer liaison between the two organisations which was articulated by the IORA Perth Communique of Nov 13 seeking *information-sharing and other activities with both civilian and non-civilian dimensions[78]*. This requires to be taken forward.

➤ **Indo Pacific Connects- Trans Ocean Groups.** There are many organisations that have an indo Pacific Character today. ASEAN, ARF, ADMM+,EAMF and EAS are more or less split in the middle between IOR and Pacific. Similarly, APEC-IORA, the trans-ocean blocks and IONS-WPNS has common members, all of which are informal ambassadors of Indo Pacific idea. They are tabulated below:-

ARF		ASEAN		ADMM+ EAS+ EAMF		IONS - WPNS	APEC - IORA
Pacific	IOR	IOR	Pacific	Pacific	IOR	Common nations	
13	12	5	5	10	8	9	7

Table 2. Existing Organisations with Indo Pacific Character

Lessons from Piracy for Future Structures

The major recent crisis in IOR is piracy. Its genesis and containment offers insights regarding future security structures. Piracy cost the world 2-6 bn US$ annually shared by industry and state as per analysis of studies by the centre *Ocean without Piracy*[79]. Piracy was finally controlled by several task forces and surveillance centres[80].

- The task forces have been:-

    - US Navy's Task force 151,

    - Additional tasking to Task Force 150(Global war on Terror TF)

    - Operation Atalanta by EU

    - Operation Ocean Shield by NATO

    - Independent deployments by Russia, Malaysia, Japan, China and India

    - Rise of private security firms and armed guards on vessels.

- The monitoring mechanism include:-

    - Contact Group on Piracy off the Coast of Somalia(CGPCS) in New York

    - The Shared Awareness and Deconfliction (SHADE) initiative meetings in Bahrain

> ➤ Regional Cooperation Agreement on Combating Piracy and Armed Robbery against Ships in Asia (ReCAAP) in Singapore

> ➤ Piracy Reporting Centre (PRC) of the International Maritime Bureau (IMB) in Malaysia

> ➤ Maritime Security Centre, Horn of Africa, London

> ➤ NATO Shipping Centre (NSC), London

The effort brought together at least 30 navies from across the globe with coordination centres spread half way across globe on a yet unfinished innings. The lesson learned towards an IOR structure is that a

> ➤ Failed state on land and abuse of sea can wreak havoc to global commons

> ➤ Resolving a similar problem can involve a fairly large force(probably the largest since World War II)

> ➤ It can take over a decade plus to push back the scourge.

The Future Structure of IOR

The following conclusions can be drawn regarding future structures of IOR:-

- **Distributed Architecture**. As Asia and Africa rises economically, there will be a need for indigenous maritime security structures to evolve and deal as first responders to a challenge. Regional organisations in IOR have the potential to initiate sub-regional maritime security regimes. It is opined that rather than creating any de novo structure, enhancing maritime awareness in existing constructs is the best way to enhance Maritime Security. The Expanded ASEAN Maritime Forum is a good model. It is such a **distributed architecture** which will provide maritime security. Given the diversity of IOR, a pan region organisation where countries find a shared traditional threat appears distant. The problem cannot be simplified. IOR

-IONS constructs can provide the 'maritime layer' to existing constructs.

- **Addressing Issue of Scale**. The efforts to deal with piracy, throws some light on the scope and scale of the problem given the size of IOR. The SAR efforts for MH307 have reiterated *that* large scope. Given that scope, a monolithic, homogenous IOR structure of security is professionally ambitious. The mandate and capacity will remain in diffused littoral organisations. Littoral organisations have to contribute collectively, where the whole, tends to be larger than its sum.

- **Inclusive Structures will benefit**. US will remain the preeminent power in IOR, and will continue to play a critical role in near term. What happens to Middle East without US power is worth pondering- Japan is already in Djibouti and China is in the process of getting there. Middle Powers like India, Australia, Indonesia and South Africa remain at pole positions in the IOR littorals. China, Japan and Korea play a key role in both Oceans. Russia is back on the block with Syria. An **inclusive structure will benefit** from their presence. IORA and IONS have that presence.

- **Funding and Governance**. It is these countries mentioned in para above who have to take the lead for funding and collective governance of structures. When we consider the Indo Pacific, the triangular relations between India, China and US becomes extremely critical to the region- a greater understanding of each other's concerns is good for Indo Pacific.

- **Watch out for Next Somalia**. Root of the problem will remain on land as illustrated by piracy off Somalia. It was a failed state on land that led to abuse of sea that seeded the piracy trouble that the world is still dealing with. If one scrapes the surface of terrorism at sea, the conclusions will be similar. Half the prospective *failed states* exist in IOR. IOR structures have to constantly gaze and respond to emerging situations in littorals.

- **IORA-IONS Onus of Maritime Layer**.   Given their pan ocean character and inclusiveness, IORA and IONS together has the potential to contribute to Maritime Security. Following measures can enhance its role.

  - ➢ **Funds and Initiative**.   The emerging IOR powers namely, India, Australia, Indonesia and South Africa will have to infuse greater energies to create consensus, generate funds, build capacity to take IORA-IONS construct forward.

  - ➢ **IORA-IONS as Maritime Twin**. It is important that both organisations exist as interrelated but separate entities since the membership and mandates do not have total overlap. However there should be greater linkages between these organisations if the spirit of IORA's Perth communique is to be taken forward.

  - ➢ **Next Way Points**. Following 'way points' are recommended for IORA- IONS construct.

    - ▪ HADR table top exercise followed by exercise

    - ▪ A central web based IOR portal for sharing assets for HADR similar to SAARCs disaster knowledge portal.[81]

    - ▪ A central data fusion centre of shipping for IOR

    - ▪ Sharing of intelligence and domain expertise.

  - ➢ **Role for Coast Guards**.   Since non-traditional security occupies a high share of the spectrum, Coast Guards have a major role as domain specialists. Whilst an Asian Coast Guard conclave exists, there is **'forum-gap'** in IOR which requires to be filled either under IONS or separately.

- **Safe Commerce- a Motivator**.   Collective security is about creating consensus. Good maritime order which facilitates commerce can serve as a strong motivator for consensus to IOR nations which are placed on the bottom of the growth curve. IORA and IONS can serve as maritime evangelists between the many littoral organisations creating a pan ocean consensus about maritime security.

Conclusion

From the perspective of commerce, the **west line**, a fictional line that tracks the historic trajectory of global centres for maritime commerce, commenced its westward journey five thousand years ago from the North Western shore of Indian Ocean[82]. Today it has traversed three fourth of the Globe and is hypothetically located in the Western Pacific. The natural progression of the west line is to the Indian Ocean, where the centre of maritime economy will eventually shift. The locus of West line is also the economic centre of gravity of the globe. That gives the IOR a unique economic gravitas in the future. Maritime Security is a prerequisite for that shift in centre of gravity. The challenge before us today, is to forge a peaceful condition amidst interplay of a wide spectrum of factors to usher that line of prosperity into IOR.

Valedictory Address

Vice Admiral Satish Soni, PVSM, AVSM, NM, ADC (Flag Officer Commanding-in-Chief Eastern Naval Command)

I must thank the USI for inviting me to deliver the Valedictory Address. It is an honour to be following such an eminent group of speakers.

The broad theme of the seminar is familiar indeed, geo-politics in the Indo-Pacific is a subject that is being studied and researched by several think tanks. However, I must acknowledge that the organisers have done well by planning individual sessions in a somewhat different manner. It was refreshing to hear the historical perspective being covered in the very beginning, and the other papers were sequenced such that one line of discussion followed the other quite seamlessly.

I must compliment various speakers for putting across their thoughts in a very logical and lucid fashion. From the papers presented during the Seminar, it is clear that most of you consider the Indo-Pacific region to be a potential flashpoint and it would be fair to presume that this could well be the thought process in the respective governments as well. Earlier this year, the National Maritime Foundation had organised a Seminar on the same theme at Visakhapatnam. It was evident then, as it is now, that the issues are complex and solutions somewhat hard to come by.

One thing that is fairly obvious that today this region is experiencing a wave of 'Maritime Nationalism'. There are several indicators towards this – development of infrastructure on disputed islands and territories, unilateral declaration of Air Defence Identification Zones, nationalisation of disputed islands, a distinct hardening of stance in Defence White Papers, forays of navies into distant waters, strident reactions to EEZ transgressions–perceived or otherwise, reinterpretation of the constitution, enhancement of naval capabilities including procurement of submarines and expeditionary platforms, and so on. Nations are striving hard to provide maritime security to their people.

There has also been a marked increase in levels of maritime cooperation – by way of bilateral and multilateral summits, exchange of arms and defence technology, joint naval exercises, staff talks, port visits and visits by service officers. For example, the Rim of the Pacific Exercise off Hawaii in 2014 saw participation by more than 45 countries; the Malabar exercise has progressively increased in terms of its scope and complexity; and there have been several 'firsts' in terms of bilateral naval exercises, the ones between India and Australia, and India and Indonesia that were held recently being examples.

Despite the fact that nations today are investing more time, effort and resources towards maritime security, and are also cooperating more than ever before, most of you predict rising tensions and increasing levels of insecurity. Indeed, this was also the prognosis during the NMF Seminar at Visakhapatnam; and I have heard a similar refrain from civilian and military officials from various countries with whom I have interacted in recent months. Obviously, the approach is less than perfect. After sitting through the Seminar, I would like to sum up my observations.

India and China are expected to take the lead in the region. Both countries have had somewhat similar experiences in the maritime domain in the past. In both cases, maritime prowess of earlier centuries did not translate into global expansion. At some point in time, both displayed a marked indifference to maritime affairs, became captive to a continental mind-set, and suffered the self-inflicted poverty of a landlocked state. Evidently, history has taught both countries a lesson, if their increased maritime orientation these days is any indication. Both would do well, however, one needs to constantly remind themselves, that the world expects them to contribute to maritime security, and not jeopardise it.

It appears that the issues, especially in the South China Sea, are not so much about conflicting territorial claims as they are about maritime security. No one country can take ownership or responsibility for ensuring maritime security, no matter how big or small an area. Maritime security has to be a collaborative effort.

Next, resolution of differences requires adherence to universally accepted conventions and laws, and a mature and sensible approach by all stakeholders. A recent example where such an approach worked quite well is the resolving of the longstanding Indo-Bangladesh Maritime Boundary dispute. Both countries accepted arbitration by a third party. The verdict may not have been in India's favour; however, it was accepted. I would say that this is a rather apt example of the 'spirit of compromise' mentioned by Dr Victor Sumsky.

Nations must avoid developing infrastructure with military connotations in their territories and in the harbours of their allies. They also need to be transparent in their actions, especially when it comes to deploying military units towards peacetime missions. For example, deploying a submarine in anti-piracy operations is difficult to justify, and is an example of an action that prompts distrust and suspicion amongst others.

Bigger nations must assess the aspirations of smaller countries and strengthen their capabilities so as to enable them to contribute towards maritime security. For example, India has gifted ships and aircraft to our maritime neighbours that are not as well equipped. We also deploy ships for patrolling the Exclusive Economic Zones of nations that lack the wherewithal to monitor their huge EEZ on their own. We do not seek basing rights, pay for our own logistical supplies, and see this purely as a benign cooperative initiative. Our training establishments today have an annual turnover of over 800 foreign trainees.

Historically, it has been seen that cooperative mechanisms take time to gain traction, especially in this part of the world. The Indian Ocean

Rim Association for Regional Cooperation – now called the Indian Ocean Rim Association is an example. Its vision was ambitious when it was first established in 1997. However, a few years down the line, its track record has been less than impressive and it still falls short of having a formal, institutionalised framework for security cooperation. On the other hand, the Indian Ocean Naval Symposium – or IONS - has done well in the relatively fewer years of its existence and has a fairly good recall value. Maybe there is a message in this that Navies ought to be offered a more proactive role in cooperative mechanisms.

Till now, IONS has largely remained a platform for discussions. I feel that it needs to be taken to the next level wherein it can play a more active role. Singapore's International Data Fusion Centre is an example where a Navy-led mechanism has been quite successful, although on a smaller scale. Recently, it played an important role during search operations for MH 370 wherein it was able to sanitise large ocean areas by tapping into its linkages with the merchant marine. Another example is that of the Malacca security mechanisms which General Dato Azizan Delin from Malaysia elaborated yesterday. A similar template could be adopted at a higher, more operational level, possibly starting with a formally established mechanism for coordinating Humanitarian Aid and Disaster Relief operations in this region. There is also the need for setting up a mechanism for intelligence sharing, especially for dealing with the threat posed by non-state actors. Indeed, there was a consensus during the seminar that this threat needs urgent, collaborative efforts.

The International Fleet Review – or IFR 16 -, with the theme 'United through Oceans', is planned at Visakhapatnam from the 5th to 8th of February 206. As of now, 47 countries have accepted our invitation, and would be represented by their ships, Chiefs of Navies and delegations. The 'Presidential Review' would involve nearly 90 ships. Other events would include an International City Parade, Operational Demo, bilateral discussions, an international Seminar, a Maritime Exhibition, and other ancillary events. Here, I must say that the response to the IFR from various Indian Ocean and Pacific nations has been extremely positive. I see this as an acknowledgement of two things – one, India's role as a key facilitator in the region; and second, of the tremendous potential that Navy-led initiatives, such as this, have for getting maritime nations on a common platform.

In the end, I would like to thank the organisers once again for inviting me. It has been a very educative couple of days, and the Seminar was conducted in an outstanding manner.

Thank you.

Concluding Thoughts

The structure and content of the seminar on 'The Indo-Pacific Region: Security Dynamics and Challenges' was to bring out need for a holistic, overarching Indo-Pacific security system and generate ideas on how it could be developed. Many different perceptions and differing views from participants across the globe were brought out. During the course of the seminar various issues came up which were discussed and views of the experts taken. Some of these are discussed in here.

A point came up as to the measures that India could take to bring the South Asian countries in a multilateral platform to fight the menace of terrorism. To this it was clarified that Terrorism is one of the threats that is affecting most of the nations in the world today. It has happened in Mumbai, Paris and could happen anywhere else. And therefore there is a greater need to focus on the type of cooperation that we need. If we do not have the cooperation in terms of intelligence sharing, if we do not have cooperation in terms of how the countries are going to deal with it, then obviously we will find the problems. That is what is going to help because whatever happens in the neighbourhood has its impact on India too and therefore, it is felt that a greater collaboration is needed on concerns of terrorism.

To a point raised regarding freedom of navigation and military activities happening in the EEZ, it was clarified that there should be no embargo on freedom through the seas. It also allows for free movement of trade and commerce through the seas that are available. Where there are issues, they will have to be solved bilaterally. In addition, international laws must take precedence in solving whatever disputes are there.

Another issue was raised that US would like to influence the Indo-Pacific region, because of economic reasons, and China is the hegemonic power in the region, so India's interest lie between China and US. How would then the strategic requirements of US be met, keeping safe the strategic and economic interest of India and China?

To this it was brought out that one does not have to exaggerate China's naval capabilities. Off course it poses a threat to Taiwan and Senkaku Island, but is not capable of challenging India or any other country in this region. China has a surplus of 3.4 billion dollars which it has to invest somewhere. In the past, it had made the mistake of investing it in the US Treasury bond, but now the only option is to put this money in some other areas. China has a strategic interest in IOR and if one combines the two then one suspects some other motives too, and it is very difficult not to suspect those. These motives may come ten to fifteen years later, however; till then it will remain a commercial activity. But one trillion dollar commercial activity is going to change the geo-political nature of the Indian Ocean Region, especially the littorals. The effect of this is what concerns India.

Taiwan's claim to Diaoyu/Senkaku Islands is identical to China but Taiwan did not cooperate with the Chinese Government. In last seven years, since communist government came to power in 2008 China did make many proposals to Taiwanese government to cooperate on the issue but there is no proof of cooperation. It was the peak of crisis but Taiwan chose to sign the fishing agreements with Japan in 2013 and not cooperate with China. Taiwan claims sovereignty over the Senkaku Island but since 2013 it has tried to solve the fishery problem first, without discussing the sovereignty issue. This position is different from China. In South China Sea, also it is the same, where there is no cooperation with China, and has still deployed coast guard forces at the reef.

It was stated that US has declared pivot to Asia, or the rebalancing to so called Indo-Asia Pacific region, and this is quite a burden, for the regional countries like Japan, South Korea, Philippines, ASEAN and even Vietnam. It was brought out that the US rebalance to Asia has two aspects; one is military and the other is economic. Until recently both were looking rather disappointing. Even today the military has not seen any earth shaking shift to the East. US has four destroyers in Singapore and one aircraft carrier additional and that's about it. As far as the economic issue is concerned, so far it was disappointing, but it is learnt that the TPP is going through with the congress, but even if it comes through, the question is – Is it going to make such a change? What China fears is that the trade between China and the US is 500 plus billion dollars and out of this 330 billion is in favour of China. So China has benefitted hugely in trade with US and made money over a decade. China fears that TPP is meant to deny that money to China. Whether it is true or not is a question mark .And it is not known whether this is going to happen in next five to ten years. May be the pattern of trade will change so that 330 billion becomes a smaller figure over a period of two to two and a half decades.

It was discussed that South China Sea to East China, there are a number of territorial disputes where in every nation has conflicting claims. In South China Sea even without China involved other countries like Taiwan and Japan have claims on Senkaku Islands. Given this kind of a situation the following issues need to be considered:-

(a) Does India's role in East Asia makes sense because making an alliance with one nation in a foreseeable future can be counterproductive because there will be other countries who India may have issues with?

(b) How far can US balance its ties with all allies in Asia, because few years back Japan and Korea had problems in East China Sea.?

To these issues the response was, that in East China Sea, India's role will be minimal, because it is too far off. Japan never conceded Senkaku as a dispute .The government never recognised it as a dispute where as China and Taiwan has claimed sovereignty over it. Can in South China Sea India play much larger role? India has extended its stay in South China Sea to 60-70 days, but Indian navy is in transition to blue water navy. India does not have a permanent presence in South and East

China Sea. However, India is in favour of freedom of navigations as 55 percent of India's trade travelled through this region.

A point was raised that there are volatile waters on the West and ruffled waters in the East and this volatility is progressing from West towards East coming as close to Arabian Sea and from East towards Andaman. In such scenario, can the waters south of Indian Ocean remain insulated from this turbulence? If no, then what is the timeframe for this turbulence to reach south Indian Ocean and what India should do to ensure that calm prevails?

The response to this was that South of Indian Ocean, there is lot of waters but no breathing ground for such volatility. The sea itself acts as a barrier because the capabilities of the small islands in the southern Indian Ocean are very limited. Further, the volatility of West is not likely to spill over to the East. But any additional PLA navy activity in Eastern sea may result in increased turbulence. One needs to be very clear about waters and bases. Every ship needs water, food and fuel which one can get from any port but a base is different where one can even get repair facilities for arms and equipment. As long as there is freedom of navigation and innocent passage, not much volatility is likely in this part of the Indian Ocean. But should the bases issue come up then the Bay of Bengal might get ruffled.

It was clearly brought out in the seminar that cooperation between the countries in this region is for mutual interest. Mutual interest is primarily economic or to fight the non-state actors and cooperation on these fronts is certainly picking up. Combined cooperation against piracy did have its effect. But is there pan IOR interest or is it only India's interest is the moot question. Now the security construct seems a non-starter if one looks through mutual interest but cooperation is also achieved by enforcement, by unipolar hegemons, by a bipolar balance of power like during the Cold War or through multilateral efforts. One needs to ponder whether a pan IOR security construct be aimed, for security or is it best left to sub-regional construct like in the gulf. While the Chinese operations in Indian Ocean are perfectly legitimate, its contours would decide confrontation or cooperation.

Possibility of a security construct between nations of the IOR seems a difficult proposition because there are some countries who also share land boundaries while others do not. But can there be cooperation against non-state actors or for mutual exploration of resources?

There have been many economic constructs but security constructs are expensive and most nations do not want to pay for security. Europe is a classic example and so, many nations invite dominant powers to undertake security. The use of force itself to ensure some sort of order is not something which most governments can do naturally. So the Indian Ocean region will see many economic and other cooperative arrangements, including against non-traditional threats but may find it difficult to see real security architecture in the region.

India today is in an excellent position to play a prominent role in the Indian Ocean Region, given its geo strategic location and the geo political developments taking place in the western pacific and the Indian Ocean Region. India should generate extra efforts to operationalize the North-South corridor. India also needs to develop proactive policies towards Maldives, Bangladesh and Myanmar.

Elements of India's Indian Ocean strategy are quite clear. India undertakes joint coordinated patrols with Indonesia, Thailand and with other countries in the East. India has also resolved issues, both in maritime as well as land boundaries, with Bangladesh. There is also in place the Indian Ocean Region Rim Association (IORA) and Initiative of the Indian Navy (IONS). These initiatives will help in economic and other soft considerations which are of interest to India and other smaller nations of the region.

It was quite clearly brought out that China's position in Indian Ocean Region and South China Sea was that it has no strategic or security aim and that Gwadar and other ports have been built for commercial reasons. However, difference of opinion does exist in South China Sea where countries have apprehensions and misperceptions.

Since there is no collective security mechanism so China is looking forward to have all stakeholders involved in establishing such mechanism, and it is not ruling out participation by any state outside this region, including of course United States, since it has a major presence in both regions. For India's role, the Chinese government keeps an open mind and since India has major maritime interest involved in South China Sea, China is not ruling out India's inclusion in establishing such a mechanism.

www.ingramcontent.com/pod-product-compliance
Lightning Source LLC
Chambersburg PA
CBHW030332270326
41926CB00010B/1593